Growing Up in
NORTHERN
PALM BEACH COUNTY

Growing Up in NORTHERN PALM BEACH COUNTY

Boomer Memories from Dairy Belle to Double Roads

RUTH HARTMAN BERGE

FOREWORD BY PRUDY TAYLOR BOARD

Charleston London
THE History PRESS

Published by The History Press
Charleston, SC 29403
www.historypress.net

Front cover, top left: View overlooking marina with the Jupiter Inlet Lighthouse in the left background, Palm Beach County, Florida. *State Archives of Florida, Florida Memory, http://floridamemory.com/items/show/59227. Photograph by Robert M. Overton.*
Front cover, bottom: ©Aerial Image of North Palm Beach Country Club by Drew Wright.
Back cover, inset postcard: Clematis Street, West Palm Beach, 2013. *Courtesy of Land & Sea Imagery. Photograph by Fred Holmstock.*

First published 2014

Manufactured in the United States

ISBN 978.1.62619.591.2

Library of Congress CIP data applied for.

To my children, Ian and Emily—to share what once was,
with all my love, for what will be.

Contents

Foreword

Reading Ruth Hartman Berge's book *Growing Up in Northern Palm Beach County* was an absolute joy. We are both Florida natives so we remember the Florida that was—a state peopled with eccentric, colorful characters and where huge expanses of unpopulated land stretched from shore to shore so that you could get on a horse and ride all day without seeing a soul. It was a gorgeous paradise strewn with palm trees and bougainvillea and guava and mango trees and a land where the pace was slower and more relaxed. In our Florida, it didn't matter whether you had five dollars or five million—what counted was whether you were a down-to-earth, decent human being.

Berge's book is a fun read, and it's also important—important because, for new Floridians, it provides insight into who we are and the forces that formed this wonderful state. This book also provides a personal record of day-to-day life. The author's love for the Florida of today as well as yesterday echoes in every line.

Whether you're a Florida native or a newcomer, you'll cherish and enjoy this book!

Prudy Taylor Board
Florida historian and author
Former president the Writers' Network of South Florida
Delray Beach, Florida
January 2014

Acknowledgements

Although writing is a solitary sport, those supporting the writer from the sidelines are many.

To Mom, Margaret Hartman; Dad, Norman Hartman; and my uncle Allen Hartman, all of whom generously shared their stories, patiently read mine and gently corrected where necessary. To my brother, John, who has constantly encouraged me. To my grandparents Gustav Hartman and Ione Hartman, my aunt Marjorie Ann Gaines Pope and my uncle Warren Hartman, all of whom have passed on but are still part of the warp and weave of my life. To Aunt Mary Hartman, Aunt Zola Hartman, Tom and Liz Gaines, Jack and Colleen Gaines, Fred and Kaye Hartman, Julieanne Riddle, Gus Hartman and Fred Hartman. To my California relatives: Ramona, Anna, Nela, Bob, Sarita and Emma. And of course, to my newly found cousin once removed or some such, Milt Longbottom. (Hooray for Ancestry.com and Facebook!)

To my teachers who always expected and demanded the best from me.

To my best friend, Becky Young, who patiently listened to my agonizing over stories for years and accompanied me to countless writer conferences, workshops and book signings. I know she's grateful this project is finally done so that she can patiently listen to me agonize over the next project.

To Larry Baker, author of several books, including *Flamingo Road* and *The Education of Nancy Adams*, who impressed me at the Florida Heritage Book Festival in St. Augustine, Florida, with both the class he taught and the class he displayed as he met and spoke with his readers.

Acknowledgements

To the author I met at a book signing for her book *Devil Eyes*, who has since become my mentor, best critic, editor and close friend, Prudy Taylor Board. Author of twenty-five books herself in the genres of history, horror and murder mystery, she has pushed me places I thought I'd never go, and I'm eternally grateful for her guidance and her friendship.

To the Magnificent Mensa Scribes; the Writers, Diners and Winers; Liz Hackney, gifted photographer and graphic artist; Rosa Sophia, former village historian for the village of North Palm Beach; Debi Murray, chief curator of the Historical Society of Palm Beach County; and Frances Hanson, director of the Historical Society of Delray Beach; Mary "Mac" Hefka, sorority sister and artistic baker with a generous heart; Fred Holmstock of Land & Sea Imagery, a genius with a camera and computer; the staff and management of the Jupiter Waterfront Inn, where I had a wonderful writer's retreat; and to those I've inadvertently forgotten to mention.

To all of you, both named and not, I couldn't have written this book without your support, encouragement and occasional kick in the pants.

Thank you,
Ruth Hartman Berge
Jupiter, Florida
October 2013

Introduction

It's been said many times that you can't go home again. In the physical sense, that's true. Landmarks are torn down or renovated past recognition. Families you grew up around sell their homes and move. It's never quite the same as you remember.

As humans, we carry the vehicle that can take us back, though. Our brains record every event that happens to us from the moment we open our eyes—some say even before those baby blues pop open. We can see something or hear a certain song, and our mind becomes a magic carpet of time travel and immediately slings us back to relive the past, to go home.

Growing Up in Northern Palm Beach County is a collection of short stories. In addition to recounting my memories, I've added some of the history of the people and places. Several of these stories were previously published in much shorter versions in my column The Florida You Don't Know, published in regional newspapers in the South Florida area by Seabreeze Publications, Inc. and on my blog, ruththewriter.blogspot.com.

The stories I've included are based in northern Palm Beach County in the towns and villages of Tequesta, Jupiter, Juno Beach, North Palm Beach, Palm Beach Gardens, Lake Park, Riviera Beach and Singer Island, where I spent most of my time. A few memories are my earliest, some are much later and all have been chosen to help show you what it was really like growing up in the paradise that was South Florida. As in most books that spring partially from the memories of the author, this book comes from the memories written in my heart. As such, there may very well be things I've remembered differently from anyone else. Any errors contained herein are mine and mine alone.

So kick off your shoes and slip into some flip-flops. Join me on the blanket I've laid out just this side of the surf line on my favorite beach here in Jupiter. Breathe the fresh, salty air and listen to the syncopated song of the sea. Let me take you home to my home that was.

CHAPTER 1

Trade You a Lake for a Golf Course

On my dresser, I have a picture of myself at age three. Smiling shyly into the camera in the 1960s, I hold a glass Coca-Cola bottle almost half as big as I am in front of my cotton sunsuit–clad body. Behind me is my dad, who is resting on a wooden picnic table bench, impossibly young and slim, his hand on my shoulder. Behind us are the pine trees and grass lawn of what was one of my mom's favorite little parks, Kagan Park. Situated on the east side of A1A, a little bit north of where the street splits off east from U.S. Highway 1 at the southern border of Juno Beach, the park sits at the south end of small Pelican Lake. Incorporated in 1953, Juno Beach was a little town in 1960 with only 249 hardy souls living in the sand dunes next to the beach, and there weren't many more by 1962, when that picture was taken. On the north end of the lake, the Town of Juno Beach built its town hall in 1991. Houses with backyards of lake instead of lawn line the western edge of Pelican Lake. To the east, a road runs between the lake and condominiums that crowd the space between the road and the ocean.

The story of Pelican Lake starts in an untitled manuscript by Charles A. Branch that I found stored in the archives of the North Palm Beach Public Library and the Historical Society of Palm Beach County while researching this book. I learned this isn't a natural lake. It's a man-made feature of the landscape that was constructed so many years in the past we've come to accept it as part of the natural scenery.

In the 1920s, Mr. Branch was hired to be the general manager of Harry Kelsey's East Coast Financial Corporation and was privy to the

Right: Author and father Norman. Kagan Park, Juno Beach, 1961. *Courtesy Hartman family collection.*

Below: Scene at Kagan Park, Juno Beach, 2014. *Courtesy Berge family collection.*

history of the area as it was being lived and created. (See Chapter 16, Kelsey City Gates, for the story of Harry Kelsey's rise and fall in northern Palm Beach County.)

In 1892, Jules Bache used to walk the golf course at the Palm Beach Winter Club (now the North Palm Beach Country Club) for exercise. Bache spoke with Branch about the golf course he and his friends E.F. Hutton and Martin Sweeny (according to linksmag.com) were going to build north of the Palm Beach Winter Club. Bache, a German immigrant who started out as a cashier at Leopold Cahn & Co., his uncle's brokerage business in New York, became the man in charge and renamed the firm J.S. Bache & Co. In the process, he became very wealthy. It's possible he might have known Sir Harry Oakes because he had interests in Canadian mining companies as well as a Bahamas-based corporation. (See Chapter 15, "The Ghost of Sir Harry Oakes," for more on Oakes.)

The three men were well known in their day. The *Palm Beach Times* acknowledges that Sweeny, a successful hotelman who was the owner and manager of Henry Flagler's residence, Whitehall, when it changed over from a private home to a resort hotel, "secured the site for the Gulf Stream Golf club and during his life-long connection with the Royal

Entrance sign to Kagan Park, Juno Beach, 2014. *Courtesy Berge family collection.*

Pelican Lake, Juno Beach, 2014. *Courtesy Berge family collection.*

Poinciana, Everglades Club and Whitehall, has shown marked executive ability and has an uncanny knowledge of Palm Beach." Sweeny was "a governor of the Palm Beach Tennis Club, treasurer of the Palm Beach Country Club, and member of the Bath and Tennis, Everglades and Sailfish clubs at Palm Beach." He served as the first secretary and treasurer of the Seminole Club and was the one to announce that even though the course and locker rooms opened on Christmas Eve, the entire club would be opening on January 7, 1932.

E.F. Hutton was the most well known of the three men, primarily because the firm he co-founded in 1904, E.F. Hutton & Co., was highly respected. Hutton started out working in a gear factory at age fifteen. He married second wife Marjorie Merriweather Post in 1920, and before they divorced in 1935, they built Mar-A-Lago, arguably one of the most beautiful mansions in Palm Beach, Florida. He died on July 12, 1962.

Branch tried to offer his services to Bache as he knew the area pretty well by then, but the three wealthy men hired Donald J. Ross, a Scottish-born golf course architect who had arrived in the United States in 1899.

Ross was renowned for golf course designs that were so well suited to the environment and topography that the courses looked as natural as if they had always been there. Shortly after Ross was hired, construction of Seminole Golf Club began.

Over the years, the club has hosted such dignitaries as President Dwight D. Eisenhower, the Duke of Windsor, President John F. Kennedy and champion golfers Sam Snead, Arnold Palmer and Ben Hogan. Most of the tournaments have been closed to nonmembers since 1961.

In the beginning, however, the three northerners and their architect knew nothing about the whimsies of the area's high tides or the periodic flooding caused by hurricanes. It was October of the first hurricane season following construction that salt water covered many of the fairways—some as deep as two feet. Branch said, "It cost them a million dollars to pump in soil to raise the course above sea level…the spoil area did create the present lake in Juno Beach."

Local historian Dan Corbett has said that Pelican Lake was dredged in 1946 by Bessemer Properties, Inc. Perhaps Bessemer added to work begun by the builders of the Seminole Golf Club. In 1946, at the same time Bessemer was working on the lake, the company built a five-hundred-foot fishing pier at the end of Mercury Way.

A ramshackle affair by the 1970s, the original Juno Beach Pier was a favorite place for my brother and I to go fishing with our dad and to sunbathe as teenagers. Standing on the end of the pier, we imagined ourselves on the deck of a pirate ship. That lasted only until the seagulls dove at our bait, and we'd run screaming like the little kids we were.

The pier operated until the 1980s, when structural damage from hurricanes proved to be fatal. It was closed temporarily by the Juno Beach building inspector. Sam Owen, an engineer who was hired to do a thorough inspection of the pier and advise Juno Beach officials if it would be possible to repair it or if it would have to be demolished. Owen believed it was reparable, and a debate ensued between Owen and those in charge. Before the debate could reach a conclusion, another hurricane came ashore, whipping high winds, surf and sand into the wounded pier, and finished the job the first hurricane had started. Owen was derided for having held the position that the pier was reparable, but had it been repaired before the second storm hit, it may very well have withstood the onslaught.

The Seminole Golf Club now sits comfortably above sea level and is a world-renowned private course still in use by members and invited guests only. Juno Beach has added more playground equipment and a few other amenities to Kagan Park, but it's still a hometown park. And Pelican Lake is still providing beautiful scenery.

The old Juno Beach Pier may be gone, but there is a newer, sturdier pier farther north. For four bucks you can stroll nine hundred feet from shore and fish out in the ocean. For a dollar, it's possible to walk out without a fishing pole to observe the sun, the sea, the beach and the bathers, surfers and fishermen, and perhaps you can imagine being a pirate while the bright blue waves crash against the pier.

The land along A1A in Juno Beach may be occupied by sprawling condominiums and exclusive private homes now, but the ocean is eternal. The sound of those waves under my feet reassure me that not everything changes. Coca-Cola anyone?

CHAPTER 2

The Dairy Belle

Sunday evenings after dinner, when we ate at home and not at my grandparents' house in Delray Beach, the talk would turn to dessert.

"Let's go to Dairy Belle for some ice cream," Dad would suggest.

"But I made lime jello," Mom would protest half-heartedly, "with fruit cocktail."

"Let the jello wait. Let's go get ice cream." He'd turn to me, all of three, to enlist my support, which, of course, was always forthcoming.

We would head out of the house to my father's convertible MG Midget and wait while he put the top down. Big hands picked me up and deposited me in the carpeted well behind the only two seats in the vehicle—no car seats or seat belts in those days. As Dad drove and Mom relaxed in the front, I spent the fifteen minutes to Dairy Belle with my face poking out beside the passenger seat. If I had been a dog, my ears would have been flapping in the wind. But no dog ever had a grin as big as mine when the wind hit my face and whipped my hair around my head.

The Dairy Belle was in Riviera Beach near the intersection of Federal Highway and Blue Heron Boulevard. A small square building of concrete block, it was covered with square tiles in a black-and-white pattern and bright pastel painted walls. We moseyed up to the window and ordered our cones. I almost always got a vanilla soft serve and pleaded for a chocolate, cherry or butterscotch dip.

Cones in hand, we would head for the concrete picnic tables in front of the Dairy Belle, where we sat and dueled with the balmy summer evening. It

The Dairy Belle, 2014. *Courtesy Berge family collection.*

was always a race to see if we were able to get more ice cream in our mouths than down our arms as the cones melted.

Mom wiped me down with wet paper napkins after I finished my ice cream, and when I was somewhat clean, I was placed back in the carpeted well for the trip home. I can still remember lying down in the well, slightly sticky despite the vigorous washing. I could listen to the sound of my parents' voices and feel the car's vibrations as Dad shifted gears to drive us home. It's odd the things that stick in your mind. The feel of that carpet is as vivid today as it was then.

The good news for you, my faithful readers, is, for once, I'm not telling you about a place that's disappeared. As of 2014, the Dairy Belle is still in Riviera Beach and still serving ice cream. The concrete tables have been replaced with metal and plastic ones, but there are still places to sit and enjoy your dessert. I can't guarantee that the cones taste as yummy as they did in 1962, but I'm sure they're just as cold and just as nice on a warm evening.

CHAPTER 3

Black-boobed Barbie and the Schweinehunds

My cousins Jack and Fred were my constant cohorts in daring escapades at my grandparents' house in Delray Beach, where the family gathered every Sunday.

Jack and Fred always brought their GI Joes. These were the full-size Joes of the 1960s—not the teeny ones Hasbro made later. (I couldn't figure out why they eventually shrunk, and when they did, they never really looked right to me.) I brought my Barbie collection. My favorite was the one with three wigs—she could be a blonde, a brunette or a redhead. The blonde wig was styled in a beehive, just like my mom's. It was a popular 'do in those days.

After making sure we said hello to all the aunts and uncles seated in the front room, we escaped to the hall and ran the "GI Joe Rescue" scenarios we loved. Unfortunately, Barbie was the perennial kidnap victim and the courageous GI Joes were forced to rescue her from the Russians, the Vietnamese or some natural disaster of epic proportions. The frozen faces of the GI Joes belied their fear as they battled bad guys and alligators or swam through treacherous rivers to rescue helpless Barbie yet again.

"Granny? Could we have a long string from your sewing cabinet?" I asked.

Granny gave us the cocked eyebrow of mild suspicion, but by then having witnessed our rescues for several years, she allowed us access to her sewing cabinet in order to liberate the perfect string to serve as a rope—all good rescues involve a rope.

Fred and I supervised as Jack looped and tied the string around Barbie's waist.

Author and brother in front of Hartman home in Delray Beach, 1966. *Courtesy Hartman family collection.*

"Don't tie it too tight," I said. The boys turned and gave me an odd look.

"It's a doll, Ruthie. There's no such thing as too tight," Jack said.

"Yeah," said Fred.

The rescues started. First, GI Joe headed into the parlor where Barbie was rescued from the jungle under Granny's hope chest and, with rope in place around her waist, was pulled to safety from evil. Then fearless Joe jumped off the stairwell at ever-increasing heights with Barbie tied to his back. When they hit the ground, poor Barbie's rescues turned into daring, dangerous pulls over the river of dark linoleum in the hallway.

Somewhere during the rescue, as I screamed, "Help! Oh, help me!" on her behalf, Barbie's outfit of the moment inevitably peeled down to her waist.

After what must have been a thousand escapades over the last few years, Barbie's perky plastic boobs were tattooed black better than if I'd dipped her womanly assets in an inkwell. She was rescued over and over and over while we ran up and down the hall dragging her, top peeled down and boobs dragging on the linoleum floor, yelling, "I'll save her!" and "We've got to get her out of this river!"

Eventually, Granddad stormed in from the front porch where he'd been sitting talking man stuff with his adult sons and my cousin Tom, who was five years older than me and didn't stoop to Barbie rescues. Granddad was over six feet tall with a bald head and glasses. His sheer size as he towered over us kept us from causing total chaos inside the house.

"*Herausmachen schweinehunds*," Granddad yelled with a sound that filled the entire house and must have been heard a block away. He marched down the hall like he was leading the charge at Normandy, his face flushed red. As he waved his fists violently in the air in our general direction, he yelled words in German we had no chance of deciphering.

"RUN!" Jack yelled, and we scattered in terror, Barbie and GI Joes trailing behind us, bouncing off floorboards, stair steps and walls as we raced to escape what appeared to be dismemberment or at least certain pain.

I don't remember any of us being swatted by Granddad, and I suspect he never would have gone for the dreaded swat on the fanny of a grandchild. Nonetheless, as we climbed over each other in our race to get out of the way of the storming, German-yelling, red-faced giant, it was clear that I wasn't the only one who thought it wise not to take the chance of being close enough to find out firsthand.

Jack and Fred raced for the nearest exit, figuring it was safest to be completely out of the house. The screen door at the back of the house smacked behind them like a gunshot and echoed, inviting another stream of German curses.

I, however, after running down the hall trying not to trip over the boys, slipped around the corner into the kitchen, where the women visited. As I stood there leaning against the wall, I panted and attempted to look like I was innocent of any possible transgression. Aunt Mary spotted me.

"Would you like to help shuck some corn or snap some of these peas for dinner, Ruthie?"

Saved from Granddad's wrath, I smiled sweetly and said, "No, thanks. I'll be back." I sidled over to Granddad's workroom at the back of the house and ducked out the screen door after the boys. I quietly closed the door behind me so as to not attract any more attention.

After I searched ten minutes through the fruit trees and hedges planted around the property, I found my cousins hiding behind the biggest mango tree in the yard. As I popped up around the tree, they reacted with wide-eyed panic and then relaxed as they realized I wasn't Granddad.

Jack said, "He would've creamed us."

Historic Hartman house, circa late 1930s. *Courtesy Hartman family collection.*

I sank down on the grass next to them, relieved that, once again, we had avoided what seemed like great danger and possible loss of limbs.

We sat in the cool grass in the shade of the mango tree and discussed the display of German temper. My cousins and I thought *herausmachen schweinehunds* was such a wonderful phrase to use when one was mad that we began yelling it at each other whenever the situation may have warranted it and, often, when it didn't even make sense.

"*Herausmachen schweinehunds*!" Fred yelled furiously as his GI Joe jumped out of the bushes to slay the bad guy yet again.

When I didn't move fast enough around the faded Adirondack chairs in a game of tag, Jack shouted at me, "*Herausmachen schweinehunds*!"

I joined in, too, as I yelled that they were both *schwienehunds* just for the heck of it.

We shouted it constantly, trying to imitate my grandfather's loud, deep, gruff voice—at least until one Sunday, when Aunt Ann, Jack's mom, overheard us. She turned white and took us aside.

Her face was serious as she informed us, "I'm sure you don't know, but calling someone a 'pig dog' in German is a huge insult. You are never to use that phrase again."

We somberly nodded our heads in agreement, even though we really didn't understand what could so horrible about being called a pig dog.

We discussed among ourselves that Germans must be awfully sensitive, as we had all heard much worse names in school. But to keep out of trouble from then on, we whispered and hissed it at each other just out of my aunt's hearing.

In my pottery class at the Arts Center in what we called the old Oakes Mansion at the North Palm Beach Country Club, I sculpted a *schweinehund.* My *schweinehund* was green and shiny and looked like a long, skinny green pig with a very crooked nose. My little fingers poked big holes for the eyes. I brought it home proudly and after my parents' confused guesses, announced that I had sculpted a *schweinehund.*

My parents looked at each other, and then my mother turned to my father and said, "I think you get to explain this one. It's from your side of the family."

I turned expectantly to Dad who just shook his head and lowered his head into his hands. "I thought Ann already explained it," I heard coming from his muffled mouth.

The next Sunday in Delray Beach, I presented my beautiful sculpture to Granddad for his approval and explained it was a *schweinehund.* He turned red and started coughing. I thought he must have been very emotional because he had no idea that I could render the mythical pig dog with such skill.

CHAPTER 4

Hurricane Memories

As I drive through the scattered debris and remnants left in Palm Beach County in 2012 by Hurricane Isaac, I think back over a lifetime of hurricane memories. Yes, I am a lifelong resident, and no, I'm not going to subject you to every memory—just a few. Promise.

During Hurricane Betsy in 1965, I set up the wondrous Show and Tell to entertain my little brother with "shows." For those of you who have no clue what I'm talking about, Show and Tell was a little box that looked like a television set with a record player on top and a slot for film. As the record played, the film, mounted in cardboard, would click from one picture to the next. Basic, I know, but it was hot stuff back then. With storm shutters over every window, the house was as dark as any movie theater I've ever been in. An added bonus of our show was that the sound from the scratchy records helped mask the eerie howl and moan of the wind.

Betsy's year was also the one a Greek banana freighter named *Amyrillis* ran aground on Singer Island on September 7 as it raced toward the safety of the Port of Palm Beach. There were thirty souls on board, and none was lost. For years—at least, it seemed that long to me—the ship was wedged deep in the sand and became an attraction that lured visitors and Florida natives alike. We swam right up to it and knocked on its sides. If anyone had ever knocked back, I think we would have fainted. While some pieces were salvaged, it wasn't until 1968 that the West Palm Beach Fishing Club towed the remaining hulk of the *Amyrillis* back out to sea to become part of an artificial reef.

Surfers in front of the *Amyrillis* shipwreck on Singer Island. *Courtesy of Palm Beach County Surfing Project.*

Fast-forward to 1979 and Hurricane David. By this time, I was a teenager and actively involved in hurricane preparations. I scrubbed bathtubs and filled them with water. Mom was in charge of dosing the water with bleach to disinfect it. I helped Dad wrap the air conditioner wall unit with garbage bags and duct tape to keep the driving rain from seeping through. We threw the lawn furniture in the pool (not recommended anymore) and lowered and secured aluminum awnings.

We hunkered down inside and stayed up as late as we could, talking and listening to the radio, flashlights close at hand. The power was usually the first casualty as the wind gained speed. We played card and board games by flashlight and lantern, the eerie shadows adding a new twist to the games. Towels were jammed under the front door to keep the rain from pouring in. The howling wind was constant until finally, blessedly, it stopped. We were in the eye of the storm—that little distance of total quiet and sunshine around which the storm winds roared. Dad opened the door and we peeked around him. Grabbing his car keys, he headed toward the marina to re-tie his boat so that it could withstand the wind that would come raging back from the opposite direction. We walked outside to give the dog a much-needed grass break and to play during the brief respite from the high winds.

Twenty minutes later, we noticed the far side of the eye wall moving toward us. The solid gray impenetrable mist that looked like a strong force was churning behind it slowly crept closer. Dad wasn't back yet. We knew he'd been through hurricanes his entire life. Born in Boynton Beach and raised in Delray Beach, he had a load of experience both in preparing for a storm and in cleaning up the aftermath. That didn't stop us from getting concerned, though. The wall slowly crept closer. No Dad. Mom made us come back in the house and start getting ready for the other side of the storm. Still no Dad.

When a hurricane first arrives, there's a build up to the action. First, clouds move in and then start zipping by faster and faster. Then, the rain starts. Finally, the storm starts to build in intensity, and the wind begins screaming around the eaves. With an eye wall, there's no build up. It's peaceful and calm and then—wham! Back in the thick of it. Just when the eye wall reached the end of our street, the sound of screeching tires heralded Dad's return. The door slammed shut behind him and he was still stuffing towels back into the doorframe when the howling winds started and rain pelted the house like rubber pellets.

As we grew up, there were hurricanes and near misses every year between June 1 and November 30. Hurricane season meant paying close attention to weather reports during those months and weeks of leftover hurricane supplies packed in school lunches after November 30.

Fast-forward to 2012. Hurricane Isaac was only a tropical storm when it passed through South Florida. Even so, it managed to dump up to fifteen inches of rain, cause flooding and power outages and spawn a tornado in Indian River County. Isaac moved on to pound New Orleans—a not-so-nice anniversary present for those who survived Hurricane Katrina.

Floridians tend to take our hurricanes as a matter-of-fact. We watch the news, stock up, board up, burrow in and wait for it to pass. Anyone who grew up along a coast in the Southeast understands that while some memories of hurricane preparations can be funny, there is nothing fun about the whine, hiss and howl of the wind and driving rain as it searches for a way to invade a shelter. There is also nothing funny about a hurricane's aftermath.

CHAPTER 5

The Joy of Terrazzo

My parents purchased our home in North Palm Beach when I was almost seven. It wasn't a particularly interesting house, but it was in a nice area and just across the village from my elementary school. We moved in a few months before my brother was born.

The house had three bedrooms, and it had something I hadn't experienced before: beautiful terrazzo floors. Many of the homes in North Palm built in the 1960s were finished with these hard, slick floors.

Terrazzo, Italian for "terraces," first became popular as a way for Venetian marble workers to use up the bits and pieces left over after installing slabs of marble. Intended as flooring for the extremely wealthy in Italy, marble chips were set in clay. Workers then rubbed the surface by hand with stones to smooth the rough spots. In the 1700s, craftsmen brought the idea to the United States, and even George Washington chose terrazzo finishes for the floors in some rooms at Mount Vernon.

Americans improved installation techniques and learned how to create patterns and different colors with marble dust. In 1924, electric grinders were first used to create a smoother finish and a higher sheen. The introduction of Portland white cement helped make even more colors available.

The terrazzo floor in our home on Jacana Way included cement and bits of marble, quartz, granite or glass. I couldn't tell you what they were, but there were little flecks of color all across the floor. Picture a birthday cake deluged with so many colorful candy sprinkles that frosting is barely visible. Another benefit in addition to its beauty and durability is that there is no cooler surface on a hot, humid Florida day. My pregnant mother often stretched out on the terrazzo to cool off in the hot fall before my brother John made his appearance. Home air conditioning started picking up in the 1950s but was still rare in the early 1960s. Central air was still on the horizon.

Marge Hartman was and is one of those fun-loving moms kids are drawn to. I was shy and quiet and often brought friends home to play with her because she had quite the sense of humor and was never too busy to entertain. Mom led our Brownie Girl Scout Troop for a while and marched with us in the Christmas in Dixie parade. Somewhere, there's a picture of her, kazoo to mouth, prancing through our living room leading a band of children, complete with party hats and kazoos. She could and would talk to total strangers in the line at the grocery store while I stood in awe behind her.

She was one of those moms who never seemed to care when I came home covered in dirt. Garden hoses took care of the worst, and bathtubs handled the rest. When I was little, she let me run around barefoot, and my feet often had black soles after a long day of tag and tree climbing. Glorious! I had three older male cousins and was a tomboy when I wasn't reading under the covers with a flashlight or acting girly playing with Barbie dolls. The ability to get dirty was something I treasured.

My cousin Jack was nine and his brother, Tom, was ten when we moved into the house on Jacana Way. They often visited. I thought they were there to play, but when I got older, I realized they were also over to give my aunt Ann, a widow, a break from the rigors of chasing two active boys.

My cousins and I hung upside down on the jungle gym in our backyard, played tag, climbed trees and made intricate forts out of the trimmings from the Florida holly tree (correctly called Brazilian pepper tree) that grew in our front yard. Trimmings were piled high in the swale by the street at least once a year. We mounded and molded the branches into rooms, the number of which depended on how many branches there were in the pile. Until the garbage trucks hauled our forts away, we sat inside on old sheets sharing secrets and stories. I remember itching all over until I could get into a nice, hot bath. We had no clue that Brazilian pepper trees are in the poison ivy family and their tree sap can cause the same reaction. They're now considered an invasive pest.

When we weren't fortunate enough to have tree fort material, one of our favorite games involved the terrazzo floor, an old blanket and my mother.

It took creative negotiating to get my mother to agree to the terrazzo game. I would agree to do the dishes or even clean my room in exchange for

Terrazzo at the West Palm Beach Turnpike rest stop, 2014. *Courtesy Berge family collection.*

half an hour of fun. At the far end of the hallway leading to the bedrooms, Mom would load Jack, Tom and me onto an old blanket and make sure we were all holding on tightly. Counting, one, two and yelling three, she'd take off toward the living room dragging us behind her as she sped up to what was surely one hundred miles an hour. The slick surface of the terrazzo was perfect for sliding.

Our favorite part of the ride was when she burst out of the end of the long hallway into the living room. There she spun us in a wide, crazy circle in the near-empty room as my dog barked at the insanity. We clutched the blanket so hard our knuckles turned white as we held on like burs sticking on a sock. None of us wanted to be the body that flew off and rolled into the drywall, though it happened occasionally.

No one ever got hurt, and no drywall was ever seriously injured in the process, though I remember laughing so hard I had trouble breathing and tears rolled down my cheeks. When I managed to open my eyes, my cousins and mom were in the same condition. We tried to talk her into it every chance we got.

One day, I came home from school to find the floor carpeted. I'm sure my parents thought it an improvement, but my cousins and I would have been happy if the floor had stayed naked terrazzo forever.

I looked into getting terrazzo installed on the first floor of the little house in which I now live because I had such wonderful memories and knew it was durable, relatively carefree flooring. It's supposed to last about forty years. I also figured I was safe from the blanket game since my kids were grown and wouldn't be begging for it.

I was astounded at the cost. I really don't think back in the early 1960s it cost the twenty to fifty dollars per square foot it does now, or it would never be lying underneath the carpets of thousands of homes throughout South Florida. Compared to manufactured wood floors that can be as low as ninety-nine cents per square foot and carpet, which, depending on the quality, can be as low as six dollars, terrazzo is a luxury in 2012.

There's terrazzo on the floor at my mom's apartment, though. I wonder if she's got an old blanket around.

CHAPTER 6

A Cheyenne Bodie of My Own

When I was six, I was in love. Deeply and irrevocably from the moment I first saw Clint Walker as Cheyenne Bodie, the title character in the TV western series *Cheyenne*. It aired from 1955 to 1963.

The show was the first western, the first dramatic series to run an hour and the first to last more than one season. Walker was six feet, six inches of lean, mean good guy, who fought every week for underdogs and against ruthless cattle barons and stagecoach robbers—occasionally sans shirt. My heart was broken when the series went off the air.

A short year later, while I was still mourning for love lost, my parents told me our family was due to expand. Mom was pregnant. I wasn't jealous of having to share the limelight with the soon-to-be sibling. I was ecstatic. Imagine. A built-in playmate!

As Mom's stomach grew under her maternity tops, I kept up by stuffing a pillow next to my bare, flat belly when running around the backyard playing with my friends—at least, until Mom caught sight of me and removed the pillow. I was asked—no, commanded—to keep the pillows outside my shirt and inside the house.

The other thing I did from the moment I learned of my impending sisterhood was tell my parents I had a name for the baby. Over dinner one night, I proudly announced that he or she should be named Cheyenne Bodie Hartman. What a wonderful idea! For some reason, however, they were not convinced. It would take more to get them to go along, and I was just the girl to make it happen.

My campaign required constant notes in pencil and crayon taped strategically around the house and in the car. It involved casually bringing the topic up in conversations, such as:

"Well, Ruthie, I think we should go to the park today."

"I like that. Cheyenne Bodie would, too."

And Mom would suddenly look at the ceiling.

By November 1965, when my brother arrived at Good Samaritan Hospital in West Palm Beach, my mother would have gladly taped me to a wall somewhere to get some peace and quiet.

Good Samaritan was all the way down in West Palm Beach, so I was deposited at my friend Sandy's house where we had a nice, giggly sleepover while my parents were busy at the hospital. At least, we were having fun until her Emmett Kelley doll ended up in the toilet. I'm not sure what the thought process was that led us to that point, but it was really funny watching his plastic head go around in circles while the toilet tried in vain to flush Emmett down. Sandy's mother was not amused.

When we woke up the next morning, I learned I had a baby brother. How exciting! My very own Cheyenne Bodie! My dad picked me up, and we rode together to the hospital, where he deposited me in the lobby with my grandparents who had driven up from Delray Beach.

In the 1960s, hospital policies did not include sibling visits. I patiently, or perhaps not so patiently, sat in the lobby with first one grandparent and then the other as each of them went up in the elevator to see my new brother. I wasn't too put out, though. Good Samaritan had a nice lobby with big windows overlooking Lake Worth. Naugahyde benches with smart silver metal legs lined the wood paneled walls, and people kept hurrying back and forth. There was plenty to see.

First opening as the Emergency Hospital on land donated by Henry Flagler near the railroad tracks, the five-bedroom cottage was quickly too crowded. "Good Sam," as the hospital was nicknamed, was built in 1920 on land that was thought to be "too far out in the swamps" during the days when West Palm Beach was a frontier town. There were only thirty-five beds in the two-story building, a far cry from the three wings the hospital was by the 1950s. Those Naugahyde benches were a relatively new decorating innovation in 1965.

I went home that night with my dad, who got the unenviable duty of breaking the news to me that they had not named the baby Cheyenne Bodie.

"But, Daddy! It was the perfect name for a new baby." I whined. "What's his name?"

"John Christopher."

"John. Christopher?" I looked at him skeptically. "You really think that's better than Cheyenne Bodie? This is going to take some getting used to."

Dad dropped me at Sandy's house again. This time our sleepover was much more subdued. Not only had Dad confessed my parents' failure to use Cheyenne Bodie as a name for the baby, but he had also been informed of our experiments with Emmett. I received quite a talking to about the inappropriateness of flushing clown dolls down toilets.

A day or two later, it was finally time to bring the baby home. I had resigned myself to the fact that he was John and looked forward to meeting him despite his moniker.

Dad pulled the paneled station wagon up to the hospital entrance, and after only a few minutes, Mom was gliding over the terrazzo floors in a wheelchair with a blue bundle in her arms. I bounced up and down on the back seat in excitement.

Mom was eased into the car and the blue-blanketed baby was gently handed to her. I leaned over the bench seat, eyes wide. She pulled the blanket off his face.

"Oh," I said.

"Isn't he cute?" asked Mom.

"Um."

"What?"

"Why is his hair black? I thought he'd be blond like me. Are you sure they didn't give you someone else's baby by mistake?"

"Yes, I'm sure. This is your brother, John."

I sat back, deep in thought. Not Cheyenne Bodie, and the hospital gave her this red-faced screaming, black-haired baby instead of my brother. She wasn't even upset. I didn't know what to think.

Dad got in the driver's side of the car, and our new family of four headed home.

Over the years, I learned a lot about having a little brother. I was seven when he was born, already in school with my own circle of friends, used to being an only child and the center of attention.

After I pestered her to be allowed to change a diaper, Mom let me assist. It was the wrong day to volunteer. The aroma coming from his diaper was not the faint smell of the narcissus. I climbed up on the step stool and pulled the diaper down. My eyebrows shot up, my eyes widened and my nostrils flared. I promptly pulled the diaper back up, climbed down the step stool and left the room. I stopped pestering after that.

Author and brother. 1965. *Courtesy Hartman family collection.*

By the time John turned two, he had learned it was fun to crash my Barbie parties. My friend Linda came for afternoon play dates and brought her dolls. We built elaborate Barbie houses and spun intricate tales of Barbie's adventures with her friends—at least, until John came into the room. He was Godzilla in a plaid jumper and bare feet. Barbies, plastic cars and clothes went flying as he smiled, happy to be involved in the play. Linda and I watched in horror until I finally unfroze and ran out.

"Mooomm! He's messing up our Barbie house again!"

Mom came down the hall and bribed John out of the room with a cookie.

We set up our elaborate house again, but this time shut the door. A short while later, John pounded on the door, and we'd hear, "Roofie! Roofie!" followed by heartrending sobs that continued until Mom came and took him. We wouldn't let him in until we were ready to put everything away. Then, his destruction was helpful.

When he was about seven, I had my first date. I was a freshman in high school and had nervously asked Mark, the cutest boy in Sunday school, to escort me to the high school choir banquet. In a long green paisley dress with flowing sleeves and lace, I looked like I had escaped from some sort of medieval reenactment. It was the height of 1974 fashion.

Mark, in a suit and tie, picked me up in his big purple 1957 Chevy complete with fuzzy dice hanging from the rearview mirror. He drove to Palm Beach, where the banquet was held in a restaurant next to the ocean. He was shy. I was shyer. I don't think we had much of a conversation the entire time. I don't really remember much about that first date. I think it was because I was traumatized upon my return home.

My date pulled the Chevy into the driveway and came around to open the car door. Remembering my charm school lessons, I delicately swung my legs together out of the passenger door and exited the car. We walked slowly to the front porch. In my head was a feverish dialog, "Will he try to kiss me? I hope he does! Oh no, do I have anything in my teeth? Maybe he won't want to!"

We stopped on the front porch, and as Mark said, "Well, good night. I had…," the front porch light went off and then on again. And as he said, "…a nice time," a voice called out from inside the house.

"Mom! Ruthie's home, and he's KISSING HER!"

A small figure in leopard-print pajamas raced away from the door.

As I slowly turned the color of an overly ripe tomato, Mark leaned over, kissed me brusquely on the lips and made a dash for the car.

There are things you don't know when you're suddenly presented with a sibling. You find out as the years roll by who this little person is. Some of us spend our childhoods convinced our parents brought a sibling home just to ruin our young lives. Siblings break our things, borrow our stuff and embarrass us. They know just the right thing to say to infuriate us. But they also defend us and love us. They hand us a flower and make us laugh to cheer us up when we're blue. When things seem bleak, they know just the right thing to say to convince us that things will get better.

So, my parents didn't name my brother Cheyenne Bodie. But as the years have rolled on, he has turned out to be every bit the hero to me that chisel-chinned Clint Walker was in that show. Even better, he's no television character. He's real. And I can reach out and hug him whenever I want to.

I just make sure he's not around when I'm getting a kiss good night on the front porch.

CHAPTER 7

S'Mores, Scouts and Summer Camp

Remember the taste of a campfire s'more? A gooey, slightly burnt marshmallow and rich melted chocolate nestled between two graham crackers? Take a bite, and as the flavors hit the tongue, rich sweetness oozes out the other side. I sure remember, and I remember where I first tasted the treat that can send me back to my childhood with one bite.

I spent parts of three summers at Camp Welaka, the Girl Scout Camp nestled between the village of Tequesta and Jonathan Dickinson State Park just over the Palm Beach/Martin County line.

These days, it's a simple drive through a nice residential area to reach the camp gates. In the 1960s, the drive took a long time as we headed into what appeared to me to be total wilderness. I was excited to finally see the two pine trees that, like sentinels, lined the road into camp. A wooden sign over the road declared that this was "Camp Welaka." *Welaka* means "chain of lakes" in Seminole. Generations of grown up Girl Scouts still smile whenever they hear that name.

The age groups are divided into different campsites on the property. The first time I camped in the woods, I was nine and in the cabins at Hillside. During my weeks at camp, the girls in my unit hiked and worked feverishly on crafts involving yards of yarn, dozens of Popsicle sticks and gallons of paint and plaster of Paris. Evenings, we gathered around campfires to sing songs like "Make New Friends (But Keep the Old)" in rounds. With the pungent smell of mosquito repellent and suntan lotion in a thick cloud around us as we sang, we sat close enough to feel the heat of the campfire on sun-kissed

Sign at entrance to Camp Welaka, Tequesta, Florida, 2014. *Courtesy Berge family collection.*

faces and toasted our marshmallows on saw palmetto stems cut and carved to a sharp point with our official Girl Scout pocket knives.

We showered in open-air showers behind high wooden fences for privacy, and the usually cold water jolted us awake. We swam and took swimming lessons in the man-made lake safely within the three-sided dock complete with lifeguard stands.

The last year I camped there I was in the tents on platforms at Outpost, the campsite farthest away from the lodge. We learned everything anyone could ever know about canoe safety in preparation for the big trip down the Loxahatchee River across the Jupiter Inlet. Only the eldest girls were allowed to brave these waters.

Girl Scouts came to the area long before my involvement. In a wonderful (but now out of print) book titled *Footprints in Time*, author Claudet Benton, herself once a Girl Scout, fills us in on the story. According to Claudet, it was January 1920 when the president of the national Girl Scouts "called a meeting at the Women's Club on Flagler Drive in West Palm Beach to organize Girl Scouting in the Palm Beaches." That meeting was followed by a national charter issued on May 5, 1920, the first in Florida. The initial troop had forty-seven teenage girls as members.

Claudet writes that Camp Welaka itself is actually the third and most successful of the Girl Scout camps in northern Palm Beach County. The first, Camp Schaum-a-Hatchee, was along the Loxahatchee, but it was destroyed by the hurricane of 1928 shortly after the first, and only, camp session. Camp Schaum-a-Hatchee was followed by Camp Margery Daniels. That camp was open from 1929 until 1935, when it closed in the aftermath of the Great Depression. Soon thereafter, concerned Scouting enthusiasts raised the necessary funds to reopen the camp, and it stayed open until the property had to be expanded in 1939 to handle the growing number of Scouts who wanted to camp there. After closing briefly in 1946 during a polio scare, the camp remained open until 1958, when the "New Site," now known as Camp Welaka, opened for campers.

Meals not cooked over a campfire were served family style to campers seated at large wooden tables in the main lodge. A stone fireplace made with stones salvaged from the fireplace at Camp Margery Daniels is the highlight of the room. Over the fireplace is a polished metal plaque mounted on the wall that carries this inscription:

> *I have given you shelter only. For the atmosphere and spirit*
> *which will prevail here you will be responsible. If you would make me happy*
> *bring from the woods the loveliest of flowers and shrubs and*
> *surround your camp with the beauty of growing things. Margery Daniels*

Around 2001, I sent my daughter to Camp Welaka, and once again, my feet trod the wooden floorboards of the main lodge. The camp has changed in the intervening years, and the area surrounding what was once a remote

Lawn in front of the lodge. Camp Welaka, Tequesta, Florida, 2014. *Courtesy Berge family collection.*

main gate now has homes in all directions. But when I picked my daughter up from her week at camp and stood with her in a song circle next to the flag post at the main lodge, my mind took a leap into the past. If I had not been holding her small hand, it could have been 1967 all over again.

There's a good reason Girl Scouts continue to exist and continue to gather at Camp Welaka. The women who started this venture in Florida in 1920 saw the future and made it happen. Then, as now, girls head into the woods to learn those wonderful things about nature that we tend not to notice as we hurry and scurry about our day-to-day lives.

Luckily, every August 30 is National Marshmallow Day in the United States. I've got some marshmallows. Who's in the mood for a s'more?

CHAPTER 8

Mosquito Coast

It seemed inevitable.

The neighborhood gang of kids I hung around with was bound to do a few foolish things at least once, maybe twice, before we turned eighteen.

Our biggest "stupid kid trick" involved the fog trucks. These were mosquito-control trucks with misting systems attached to the back that traveled around North Palm Beach (as well as most of Florida) during the rainy season in an attempt to keep the mosquito population down.

Fog poured out of the back in huge, billowing clouds. That looked cool to us, and we, totally ignorant of the toxins being sprayed, rode our bikes in and out of it, reveling in the novelty. The smell was odd, kind of bitter if we opened our mouths, but the white clouds were irresistible. Parents yelled, and kids were sent to showers and then to bed.

We gradually got the idea that riding through mosquito fog was not the brightest idea we'd ever had. But we'd still be drawn to the clouds like ants to sugar.

South Florida has always had a mosquito problem. The muck and marshes were, and are, perfect breeding grounds. After daily summer afternoon thunderstorms and the occasional hurricane, standing water provides a perfect nursery for the bloodsuckers.

The Mosquito Information Site (yes, it really exists at http://mosquito.ifas.ufl.edu/) states that many European explorers wrote about having to "sleep on the beach covered with sand" to escape the hordes of blood-sucking menaces. There was even a Mosquito County in 1824. You know it today as Orange County—home to Mickey and Minnie Mouse, living in Orlando's Disney World complex.

The first mosquito association to do battle against this formidable foe formed in 1922, according to the Mosquito Information Site. The *Lake Ida Current* carried a quote from longtime resident Haide Zelder in the spring of 2011, claiming that in the early days of the Delray/Lake Ida area, which would have been the late 1800s, mosquitoes were "so big and black, like a swarm of bees; we'd have to run!"

I've read stories that in Jupiter as well as Delray (then called Linton), residents were careful not to step out their front doors without long sleeves. In those days before mosquito control and repellents, it took mere seconds for insects to swarm and land and then pierce and feast on unsuspecting skin.

Although mosquito control is doing well in holding back the seasonal swarm, all mosquito feasting is not in the past. I recently heard about two acquaintances who, while visiting the Florida Oceanographic Institute on Hutchinson Island, were repeatedly bitten. The husband posted on Facebook, "It's safe for everyone else to visit. My wife and I made sure the mosquitoes have already been fed."

Now that I have you itching in sympathy for our ancestors who braved the hordes, let me reassure you that these days, Florida has mosquito control from helicopters. There's some controversy as to whether or not the spraying causes damage to other, less irritating, Florida wildlife, such as birds, fish and deer, but the mosquitos are, for the most part, subdued. Trucks still spray in several Florida counties, too.

As a child, I was always fascinated with the fickleness of the mosquito. The female mosquito will feast on a poor innocent person while nearby, someone else sits relatively unscathed. I'm one of the latter—happily rarely attacked. Perhaps there was a benefit to riding through the mosquito fog after all.

CHAPTER 9

North Palm Beach Elementary Echoes

One windy day in October 2012, I visited what had been my elementary school. As I walked through the halls I had raced through as a child, my footsteps echoed and wind pushed something around just out of sight. I was surprised to find the school still standing. North Palm Beach Elementary was scheduled to be demolished so that a new technologically advanced school could rise from the ashes by 2014.

Walking down the halls, I peered in windows and tried to remember what it had been like, what I had been like before life accelerated way past worrying about which friend I would sit next to at lunch. I had spent several years of my life here. Graduates I know are doctors, lawyers, magistrates, teachers, politicians, parents, artists, homemakers and writers.

It was 1965 when I was first enrolled here. Toward the end of that summer, children all over North Palm Beach met in the "cafetorium" (a name the Palm Beach County School Board used to describe the combination cafeteria/auditorium) to buy large paper sacks of school supplies from the Parent-Teacher Association. The PTA charged five dollars per sack to provide everything needed, and it was heavenly looking at all the interesting things I'd be using in the coming year.

My memories start at first grade; Mrs. Atherton was my teacher. We sat in wooden chairs at tables and used our big pencils to write in workbooks that told the story of Dick and Jane and their dog, Spot. We took their lives seriously as we labored over each letter. "Run, Spot, run. See Spot run. Dick and Jane see Spot run."

Hallway at North Palm Beach Elementary, 2012. *Courtesy Berge family collection.*

In the days before any of us knew the meaning of SPF or sunblock, physical education was held on sprawling fields that stretched to the north and west of the school. We clasped hands to play Red Rover and yelled, "Red Rover, Red Rover, send Tommy right over!" until with aching arms, sweaty bodies and bright pink noses and shoulders, we trudged, exhausted, back to the classrooms. Our bobby socks were colored gray by Florida sand and dotted with sticking burs that we picked up from the weeds in the fields.

We had a school orchestra, and I attempted to learn how to play the cello. I have no idea why I didn't choose a flute or something small, but I was very grateful that my friend Chip Mutz helped haul the cello to the curb when I had to take it home to practice. We waited for our rides under the melaleuca trees that lined Anchorage Drive, peeling the papery bark of the trees as we talked.

Author (right) and neighborhood children modeling spring celebration headgear, possibly 1967. *Hartman family collection.*

When I was at North Palm Elementary, Spring Carnival was held on the front lawn where the library was later built. We wore colored poster board cut in the shape of tulips, roses or daisies on our heads like masks with oval holes cut for our faces and ribbons holding them in place. We sang songs about spring and danced.

North Palm Beach Elementary went up in stages beginning in the late 1950s until it was as finished as it could be in the 1970s. Gradually, portable classrooms were installed on the edges of the play fields to the north, and then the portables themselves were replaced with buildings. The school disappeared much more quickly. The 2012 plans were to pull down almost all of the buildings and remodel the two that would remain. The cafetorium was to be replaced with a better facility—a nicer cafeteria and more impressive stage. I remember it as a big high-ceilinged room where suspiciously, cafeteria ladies always served spinach on days the lawn was mowed.

I really do understand that the old school was out of date. Technology has raced ahead, and the old buildings were built long before computers became small enough to fit in a phone. The price to retrofit must be much greater than the cost to just tear down and rebuild. Part of me, though, regrets that I won't be able to drive by and see how my school has changed. Unlike my father, whose school still stands as part of Old School Square in Delray Beach, mine will disappear.

Bittersweet, to be sure.

If you're a graduate of North Palm Beach Elementary, it's too late for one last visit. Demolition and clearing is over, and new buildings have risen from the dust. When I wrote this story, I'd driven by one last time to say goodbye. As I walked out of the school for the last time, the sun slowly set over what was left of the play fields, and shadows crept farther and farther down the halls. The sound of my footsteps echoed against those walls I last touched when I was eleven.

CHAPTER 10

Salvation in the Earman River

A river runs through North Palm Beach. At least I always thought it was a river. We lived close enough that it became the focus of much of my childhood lore.

The Earman River and the bridge that crossed it at Prosperity Farms Road was a major part of our landscape in the southern part of the little village of North Palm Beach. Boys gathered on the riverbanks to fish or, if they were lucky, to chug up and down the river in little boats borrowed from their dads.

Men on their way out to Lake Worth and to the Atlantic Ocean to fish would wave to kids along the banks as they made their way east, unless a dad spotted his own kids. Then it was, "Hey, is that you Ernie? I told you to stay away from the river! I told you! Wait 'til I get home! You'd better get there before I do!"

In the early 1970s, my friends and I borrowed my brother's rickety red wagon and loaded it with glass bottles we collected from the trash. After collecting as many bottles as possible, we walked to the Village Store on Prosperity Farms Road and turned them in for the recycling deposit—a fortune to us in those days. Sometimes we received as much as fifty cents for our load.

From our home, the Village Store was a half mile down Prosperity Farms Road and across the Earman River Bridge. We debated the wisdom of hiking

Earman River looking east, 2013. *Courtesy Berge family collection.*

in heat so heavy it was like breathing underwater, but we did it anyway. The lure of collecting deposits usually won.

Reaching the open garage doors of the store, we dragged ourselves across the hard-packed dirt floor into the shade, our sneakers getting dusty as we shuffled to the register. We showed our bottles to the clerk who counted them and silently pointed to the back door. We got a nickel for every bottle.

After setting the bottles inside wooden crates that were stacked outside the back of the store in organized chaos, we happily collected our quarters

The Village Store, now known as the Village Grocery, circa 1970s. *Courtesy of Tony Nasser.*

and shopped with reckless abandon. The discussion was fierce as we debated which candy to choose—Chick-o-sticks, bubble gum, candy cigarettes? And this time, should we get some of those little wax bottles with the way-too-sweet syrup inside or not? At the end, we added a Coca-Cola in a big glass bottle. Happily we left the store, carefully carrying brown paper bags containing our reward for being good recyclers.

We took turns dragging one another and our bags filled with goodies in the wagon on our way back to the Earman River Bridge. There, we pushed the wagon behind the bushes for safekeeping and slid down the steep sides of the riverbank to the cement wall under the bridge, where we sat in the cool shade. Dangling our feet over the water and slowly feasting on all that sugar, we savored every illicit bite.

Without our mothers looking over our shoulders making dire predictions of horrible future dentist visits, we ate our newly purchased candy in peace. In front of us, the brackish water of the river barely moved. Every now and then a fish appeared just below the surface like a marshmallow trying to pop out of a bowl of warm molasses, but not quite making it.

When I was ten, I decided I was going to live under the Earman River Bridge. Convinced as only a drama queen in training can be, I was sure I had been mistreated and was unappreciated. My parents obviously didn't deserve such a wonderful daughter. My refusal to eat another Brussels sprout was not a reason to send me to my room.

So late one night, I pushed out the screen of my big front window and crawled over the bushes, obtaining several scratches from the freshly trimmed branches. It was around eight o'clock and newly dark when I stomped off toward my new home under the bridge muttering a few choice words. I stormed down the sidewalk. The cool October wind lifted my hair as if fingers twirled my blonde locks and puffed up my thin cotton nightgown before sucking it back against my body.

"I can live under the bridge, and my friends can bring me food," I decided. "That'll teach 'em."

It was a great idea that got better and more elaborate in the details as I got closer to the river—until I reached the corner of my street and noticed it was dark, very dark.

I stopped and looked around. There was a slight twisting in my stomach. Something in the neighbor's yard rattled. Eyes wide, I peered into the darkness. One more bang rang out from farther down the street, and I turned and raced back to the house, climbed back in the window, dove in the bed and under the covers. There would be no living under the bridge anytime soon for me.

Once, my cousin Jack raced toward the Earman River for salvation. It was a family tradition to grab whoever was close to you when they least suspected it and rub your knuckles on their scalp while screaming, "Noogie!"

Jack, with the arrogance of a teenager, made the mistake of daring my dad to give him a noogie late one Saturday afternoon just as the sun started to drop behind the trees. I think his exact words were, "Well, you can't catch me, old man." The two of them stood frozen looking at each other.

Time seemed to expand. The breeze stopped. Leaves stilled. Birds stopped chirping.

My dad twitched a finger, and Jack exploded. He dashed across the yard and over the fence. More surprising, my dad did the same. The rest of us turned to one another, mouths open. None of us had ever seen either of them move that fast.

They didn't return for a half hour, and both came back panting. Jack hadn't stopped running until he reached the Earman River. Thinking he might swim to safety, he hesitated a brief moment before diving in that murky water, and that's where Dad caught him.

On the banks of the Earman River, Jack was given the much-deserved noogie.

The water of the Earman River was brackish and dark brown, and our parents spent a lot of time warning us to stay away from it. I had no idea what was on the bottom, and I doubted if any of my friends did either. Boys dared each other to swim from one side to the other, but I, along with my girlfriends, refused to get that close.

I heard once that a shark had been sighted in the Earman, which sent most of the kids into a shark-hunting frenzy. After weeks of campouts and daily meetings where binoculars were handed around along with a thermos or two full of Kool-Aid, we had failed to sight even the bare tip of a shark fin. We finally became highly suspicious that there was no shark.

Numerous discussions were held about whether anything other than a muck monster or perhaps a mullet could live in that dark water. Discussions became hot debates about whether the shark story may or may not have been invented by a parent who had finally lost patience with his kids coming home reeking of the river.

I know now that the Earman River wasn't even a river. Natural rivers in Florida tend to meander peacefully and lazily back and forth like the respectable Suwannee or St. James River farther up state. I never noticed that the Earman is remarkably straight.

Years after spending all those summer hours under the bridge and shark hunting along its banks, I finally learned Earman is a man-made canal, built in 1897 to help with drainage for the farms that were in the area way before North Palm Beach even existed. Joseph Borman, Elisha M. Dimick and George Lainhart started digging it by hand. These three men later became very important in the settlement of early Palm Beach County. Borman became the first town marshal of Palm Beach (the town, not the county); Dimick, who had already served both as a state representative and senator, became the first mayor of Palm Beach; and Lainhart, who came to the area as a carpenter, ended up providing building supplies to Henry Flagler. Lainhart later teamed up with George Potter to found Lainhart & Potter, a building supply company that remained in business until the family sold it in 2012—a remarkable run of 119 years—to Marjam Building Supply, a New York firm.

Equipment eventually came into the picture in the digging of what was first known as "Dimick's Ditch," or the three would have been digging forever. As it was, the canal was completed before 1900.

The cool bit of shade and concrete under the bridge was our oasis away from the summer sun, our hideout from our parents and pesky siblings. The hours we spent lying on our backs munching candy with the roar of an occasional car swooshing by on the paved bridge overhead were filled with talk of what we were going to do and who we were going to be when we finally grew up and could move away from home.

It shouldn't have been a big surprise when one of the boys grew up to play with sharks. Jim Abernethy has spent most of his adult life diving among them and has become a huge advocate for shark conservation. Come to think of it, I suppose it could have been Jim's dad who started the rumor that kept us busy and out of trouble that summer.

So there's a river running through North Palm Beach. Started with a shovel, it survived while the farmland around it sprouted houses. I'm sure today's children are still spinning stories on the mucky banks of the mighty Earman as the mud squishes through their toes.

CHAPTER 11

Hetzel Brothers Christmas

If you've ever spent a Christmas in Florida, you know it's definitely not like a northern Christmas. In St. Louis, for example, while there may or may not be snow on the ground, it's always cold enough in December for a roaring fire in the fireplace.

Not so in Florida. As a child, I didn't realize what I was missing. Sure, it sometimes got cold, but often as not, Christmas Day dawned a balmy seventy degrees with bright sunshine. No sledding. No snowmen. No snow. But before anyone from north of the Mason-Dixon line feels sympathy for us, let me assure you that there were and are advantages, too. Chief among them, the ability to take a new skateboard out for a test drive or head over to the beach with a surfboard from Santa for a couple hours or to soak in the sun—on December 25.

One of my favorite Christmas memories began before my bare feet ever hit the Florida sand. The Hetzel Brothers Christmas Pageant became an annual tradition for my family as well as many other families in Palm Beach County. Originating in little Nashville, North Carolina (no, not Tennessee), in 1933, the display of papier-mâché figures was arranged to tell the story of the Nativity. The brothers moved south to Palm Beach County, where they settled in Currie Park next to the water in West Palm Beach. It was the late 1960s when the annual event moved to the corner of Northlake and MacArthur Boulevards in Palm Beach Gardens.

I remember it as always chilly the night we joined the crowds that walked through the production. Dad parked the car in the fields behind

Hetzel Brothers display, possibly 1970s. *Photograph by Harry Wright.*

the rocks, and we walked up to the entrance. All the Floridians were bundled up as if it were the dead of winter in the South Pole instead of fifty degrees. Northerners were easy to spot because they were the ones in short sleeves. We put a dollar or two in the donation box—there was never an entrance fee—and joined the line moving slowly past the dramatically lit figures depicting scenes of the birth of Christ. Over the years, the recording of the narrator reading the story at each scene became scratchier and even skipped from time to time, but we patiently and faithfully listened anyway.

Fourteen years after arriving in Palm Beach Gardens, Bob Hetzel closed the gates and turned out the lights. He had suffered a heart attack, the pageant was in financial trouble and the city, responding to complaints from residents, had been pressuring Hetzel to correct electrical problems. Hetzel had been directed to move the buildings on the site after that year's Christmas display. It was time. There was no fourteenth production, and the pageant folded in 1983.

These days, when you drive by that intersection, you'll see nothing unusual. No rocks piled high. No papier-mâché angels glowing against the night sky and palm trees. No faint Christmas carols on the winter breeze. Nothing remains to suggest that it was once the site of an endearing Christmas—and Easter—tradition for families in the area. There's nothing left there of the costumed figures.

Thanks to the generosity of fellow history enthusiast and Palm Beach Gardens Historical Society chairman Don Kiselewski, I spent an evening lost in memories as I viewed the DVD presentation Don and his granddaughter, Kelly Chase, prepared for the Palm Beach Gardens Historical Society. If you grew up visiting Hetzel Brothers Pageants, make a point to see this if it's ever presented again.

You can even pretend you're standing shivering in the field and listening to the scratchy recording of the narrator of old.

CHAPTER 12

Dolphins, Girl Scouts and S&H Greenstamps

In the 1970s, when a Girl Scout was old enough to camp at the Outpost campsite in Camp Welaka in Tequesta, there was one event that every camper anticipated—the canoe trip south on Loxahatchee River and across Jupiter Inlet.

The camp is nestled along the shores of the North Fork of the Loxahatchee, a slow-moving river that, in 1985, earned designation as a Federal Wild and Scenic River. One of only two such rivers in the state, it's also the last free-flowing river in South Florida. Only the eldest campers—the just-barely teenagers, who had received years of canoe safety courses—were permitted to participate in the daylong expedition.

The year I "came of age," we piled in canoes and, for the first mile, paddled energetically south down the North Fork. Cypress trees rose out of the water, dripping with Spanish moss. It was beautiful to look at, but no one wanted to drift into it. The chiggers that infested the moss transformed anyone who got into it into a miserable itching pile of flesh. Turtles sunned themselves on fallen logs along the way, and every now and then, we spotted a gator. Birds flew around the river—herons and blue jays among them. It's been said that the North Fork is one of the little corners of Florida that looks much as it did when settlers first moved into the area.

Grateful for the current, we Scouts followed the fork to a central embayment area. We traveled to the east to Jupiter Inlet and the open ocean. When we finally arrived at the inlet, a trip of around two river miles,

View looking toward the Loxahatchee River at Jonathan Dickinson State Park, Hobe Sound, Florida, circa 1900s. *Florida Department of Tourism, State Archives of Florida, Florida Memory, http://floridamemory.com/items/show/91326.*

View of Jonathan Dickinson State Park visitors canoeing near docks at Hobe Sound, Martin County, Florida, October 1960. *State Archives of Florida, Florida Memory, http://floridamemory.com/items/show/57868. Photograph by Charles Barron.*

the current rushing out to sea became more difficult to row against. We dug our paddles hard into the water to avoid being dragged by the current out of the inlet and into the ocean. Alongside our canoes, dolphins cavorted as if they could sense we were nervous about the threat of the open ocean to our left and wanted to escort us to safety. They were so close we could see the texture of their skins. Their smiling faces encouraged us, and we knew we could reach the other side.

Once across, we made landfall at Suni Sands, a mobile home park that sits between State Road A1A and the water. There, we enjoyed a picnic lunch of sandwiches, punch and cookies set up by the camp counselors while we sat on the manicured lawn in tired clumps of sweaty girls.

It wasn't until 2011 that I learned Suni Sands Mobile Home Park is located on top of a prehistoric Indian village site—a rare "double platform mound." Traditionally, these mounds were reserved for the chiefs with the most prestige. In fact, the entire area around the inlet is a treasure-trove of Indian artifacts.

The Suni Sands property was at one time owned by William and Emily Sperry of S&H Greenstamps fame. Greenstamps were the housewife's friend beginning in 1896. Women earned stamps as they bought groceries and licked and pasted those little stamps into books. They collected stacks of books until they had enough to redeem the small green books for items of their choice. My college roommate and I practically furnished our dorm room with S&H Greenstamp products.

Sperry loved boating and fishing. He ended up in Jupiter when his wife, Emily Sperry, purchased the property along the inlet and built their home, which bore the title of "Winter Estate," in the late 1890s. Mr. Sperry later added a boathouse and ballroom for entertaining.

In the late 1800s, the main entrance of Suni Sands was the roadbed of the northern terminus of the Jupiter and Lake Worth Railroad, better known as the Celestial Railroad because the train made scheduled stops at Venus and Mars with a southern terminus in Juno. There was nowhere to turn around, so the train backed up from Juno for the return trip to Jupiter. It wasn't unusual for the engineer to stop the train so that gentlemen passengers could shoot at wild game spotted from the railway cars.

In the 1940s, the area became Suni Sands Motor Park with a Sinclair gas station next door. The motor park remains, but the gas station is now Schooner's, a seafood restaurant.

Close by to the east is DuBois Park, which was once called "Stone's Point." For two years, the point had been occupied by a Major Stone (his first name is lost in history) and his crew, who were trapped in the inland waterway when their ship was forced to take shelter there in a storm. The inlet closed when the storm rearranged the sand, trapping the ship and requiring them to wait it out. In the *Courier Highlights* published on May 23, 1974, the story goes that the ship was a charter from New York that Stone sailed to Jupiter. He had a grand plan to sell palmetto logs for Key West dock construction; however, while the ship was inland, the inlet closed, and both the ship and its cargo rotted. Stone? He apparently decided walking was the only way out of his situation. He walked north on the beach all the way to Canaveral—a distance of 124.5 miles.

It was 1892 when Harry DuBois arrived and purchased the point. A native of New Jersey, Harry ended up in Florida working on Flagler's Royal Poinciana Hotel and later as part of the Jupiter lifesaving crew captained by Charles Carlin. He liked the area, and Stone's Point was his second purchase of land. It's been said he admired the Indian shell mound that ran from the northwest to the southeast across the property. It had been believed that the huge shell mound was a midden, or Indian trash heap, but excavation points to the possibility that the mound was an architectural feature built for the residence of Indian chiefs and their families. Scrapers, sharp points, knives, various items carved from greenstone and pottery shards have been found among the oyster shells.

For years, DuBois lived in a little shack he had floated down the river to his property. When he finally built the DuBois house in 1898, it was on top of that huge shell mound. About two-thirds of the ancient mound was sold and carted south to create roadbeds in Kelsey City (now Lake Park). The big mound the house currently sits on is but a small portion of the original approximately six-hundred-foot mound. It's still possible to see a gentle swell to the landscape where the remaining mound is located. What's left is protected as a historic and archaeological treasure.

When we were children, Mom's favorite spot for family picnics was on a corner of Jupiter Inlet Park next to the little footbridge that crossed to DuBois Park. The tall Australian pines provided shade for the concrete picnic table and benches. Shade was a necessity for a long day at the beach. Without it, painful sunburn was a real possibility.

The footbridge crossed over a small, fast-moving stream. When the tide was coming in, water rushed under the bridge and into the estuary behind it. We jumped off the bridge and floated on the current until it grew too weak to carry us. When the tide was going out, we waded in the shallow water until we could barely feel the tide sucking at our legs. Then we flopped down on our backs and floated, letting the tide carry us out to the bridge and the inlet beyond.

My friend Kelly Farrell, who grew up in Lake Park, asked me if I remembered when the DuBois family still lived on the property. A member of the family would come to the road when cars pulled up, and as Kelly and her brother, Kip, hung out the windows, the Farrells were charged a dollar for the carload to park and enjoy the beach. DuBois Park was another one of my family's favorite places to picnic in the late 1960s and '70s.

You can drive by Suni Sands today, but there's no entry. It's private property. DuBois Park is now part of the Palm Beach County Parks and Recreation Department. The pioneer home of the DuBois family, first restored by the Loxahatchee River Historical Society in the early 1970s, was severely damaged in 2004 and 2005 when Palm Beach County suffered through three hurricanes in a row (Jeanne, Frances and Wilma), and repair and restoration is ongoing thanks to the generosity of the Loxahatchee Guild.

DuBois Park itself is open to the public, and you don't even have to have a spare dollar.

And if you're wondering, we Girl Scouts, after a hearty lunch, dragged ourselves back to the canoes for the trip back up the North Fork to Camp Welaka. The tide was against us, and the trip took twice as long. By the time we arrived back at Camp Welaka, our arms were rubbery, and we were exhausted. But we were proud—we had accomplished the first canoe trip of our lives and hadn't had to be rescued from the ocean by the Coast Guard.

CHAPTER 13

Halloween Memories

On Halloween in 2011, the kids danced between raindrops while they clutched their costumes, hats, masks and goody bags. It was another windy Halloween in Florida. As far back as I can remember, Halloween was always warm, windy and spooky. The dry rattle of palm fronds high above the street combined with the dance of light and shadows caused by the tropical full moon were enough to cause little hands to clutch flashlights and goody bags with equal tension.

When I was a child, we created our own costumes out of our parents' closet castaways and then added a couple of store-bought touches, such as vampire teeth, a scary monster mask or a tiara. We crossed neatly manicured lawns of St. Augustine grass, knocked politely on doors and yelled, "Trick or treat." The resident who was lucky enough to answer the door leaned out with a huge bowl of candy. As they oohed and aahed over our costumes, they dropped candy in our bags. We yelled our thanks and ran to the next house.

The year I was six, my mother was pregnant with my brother, who was born on November 3, three days after Halloween. She answered the door, and the eyes of the trick-or-treaters grew huge at the sight of her gigantic belly. My brother always did know how to steal the show.

When I moved to St. Louis with my husband and our son in 1994, I learned that other areas of the country did things slightly differently for Halloween.

On our first Halloween in the Midwest, for example, we dressed our eighteen-month-old son as Batman and took him trick-or-treating with his

Brownie Girl Scout Troop Halloween party, 1965. *Courtesy Hartman family collection.*

cousins. I soon discovered that in St. Louis, when you knock on a door, you have to have a riddle ready. The riddle is asked, an answer attempted and then the candy dropped in your treat bag.

At the first door the kids approached, the unsuspecting homeowner opened the door, and our young son marched right in the house, down the hall and disappeared. We stood there with our mouths agape as we watched him go. Then we started calling, but whatever he had found in the room at the end of the hall was much more interesting than we were at the moment. Finally, our niece was invited in to collect him. She found him sitting next to the bemused man of the house, both watching a football game on television.

After I returned to Florida several years later with a daughter as well as the Batman wannabe, I would take my two around a nearby neighborhood—one with a large number of homes. Kids ran all over the place, hysterical on candy highs from smuggled sweets crammed in their mouths between houses. The wind was still causing the palm fronds to crackle. As crazy as it got, even when we had walked so far we could no longer feel our feet, it was still fun.

When my children were still little enough to enjoy going trick-or-treating with mom, we always ended up at the home of my grandmother and aunt.

By then, the children were exhausted, make-up was smudging off their faces and their costumes were askew, but my grandmother and aunt always made a fuss. My kids were always thrilled and proud that they had "scared" the two elderly ladies with their costumes.

My grandmother and aunt have been gone several years now, and my children are adults. Funny, I used to think it would be the big things I'd miss when my children were grown. I never thought it could be the mad scramble for the right costume, aching feet, arguments over candy or laughing at the can of soda someone gave out as a treat one year because they ran out of candy.

I missed all that fun and excitement when I sat alone at last on Halloween, listening to the whistling wind and rustling palm trees while quietly reading a book as I waited for one little trick-or-treater to find his or her way to my door.

CHAPTER 14

Tumbling Down Lighthouse Bridge

In the 1960s, children spent a lot of time on bikes in North Palm Beach. We rode back and forth from one another's houses, the North Palm Beach Country Club pool and Anchorage Park. We also rode for business. Children delivered papers, sold Girl Scout cookies and traveled to and from North Palm Beach Elementary as soon as we were able to talk our parents into letting us.

North Palm Beach was a small town then. It was not quite six square miles in size, and a little more than a third of that was water. Population was a scant 2,684 in 1960, and everyone knew everyone.

When North Palm Beach was in the planning stages, John D. MacArthur, a wealthy entrepreneur and local developer, decided he wanted to have as many homes as possible on the water. As a result, North Palm Beach has canals going every which way and a high percentage of waterfront property.

MacArthur was a legend in Palm Beach County. His brother, Charles MacArthur, became a famous playwright, but John MacArthur's path to riches was through insurance. Born dirt poor, he became rich in the insurance industry beginning with his purchase of Bankers Casualty & Life for $2,500. In 1954, MacArthur was already deep into Florida real estate when he bought 2,600 acres of land that had previously been owned by Harry Kelsey and then by Sir Harry Oakes. The land he purchased included most of today's Lake Park, North Palm Beach, Palm Beach Gardens and Palm Beach Shores.

Lighthouse Bridge, North Palm Beach, 2014. *Courtesy Berge family collection.*

An eccentric in his later years, MacArthur was well known for conducting business from a table in his Colonnades Beach Hotel on Singer Island. Find a local who was around in those days, and you can get an earful of stories. MacArthur and his second wife, Catherine, lived upstairs in the penthouse until his death in 1978 at age eighty. They also owned a small, unpretentious house in Lake Park.

To reach Anchorage Park or the elementary school from our house on Jacana Way (near Lighthouse Baptist Church), it was necessary to go over the Lighthouse Bridge. Built in 1958, the bridge was a challenging 104 feet to young bike riders on Lighthouse Road, the first main east–west thoroughfare through the village.

We were supposed to walk our bikes over the huge, steep hump, but when school wasn't in session, no one was there to make sure we obeyed the stenciled "Walk Your Bike" command at the foot of the bridge. We often deigned to trudge up the steep hill walking our bikes, but once at the top, we jumped on and glided down, wobbling at high speed. Kids often wiped out at the foot of the bridge and hobbled away with scraped knees and banged up bikes.

One of the attractions on the other side of the bridge was the summer camp at Anchorage Park. It was a casual camp that lasted a week or two.

Most of us had moms at home in those days, but if other moms were like mine, they enjoyed having a couple of hours of peace and quiet in the middle of the summer. We had handmade nametags with our names spelled out in macaroni and spent a lot of time playing games in the heavy heat all over the twenty acres of grass or resting on the benches at wooden picnic tables trying to catch our breath. Camp counselors were teenagers, and there undoubtedly was an adult or two around. Kool-Aid was the beverage du jour, and we swilled it by the gallon, leaving our lips bright red or orange.

We spent a lot of time on those acres when camp wasn't in session, too. On a Saturday or a free day in the summer, once we arrived at Anchorage Park, we threw our bikes on the ground and raced for the big swings that sat parallel to Anchorage Road close to huge shady ficus trees. Swinging with wild abandon, we launched ourselves into the sky at the optimum moment to catch the most air before we sailed toward the ground and rolled upon landing.

We ran to the merry-go-round. A simple metal affair, it had railings so children could hang on while their parents sedately pushed the ride around. My friends and I, though, didn't believe in doing things sedately. If there were no little children riding, a couple of us would hop on and lie down flat on the warm metal. We wedged ourselves up against the railings. One friend would dig her feet into the sand and race faster and faster, almost falling face down in the dirt to make the merry-go-round turn as fast as possible. When the ride slowed to a stop, we fell off the sides and staggered away into the grass where we collapsed to watch the clouds and trees spin above us.

"Ohhh," one would always say, "I think I'm gonna be sick!"

"I can't believe we got it going that fast!" another would reply.

"Let's do it again!"

And we did.

Most of the time we were still slightly dizzy when we staggered back to the merry-go-round for another ride, laughing and giggling at the sheer delight of acting so silly.

When we had enough of riding in circles, we ran over to the zip lines. In those days before litigation lotto took control of the

Warning at the foot of the bridge, 2014. *Courtesy Berge family collection.*

country, Anchorage Park had two big metal posts buried deep in the ground around thirty feet apart. Each post had an almost completely enclosed metal cage surrounding a metal platform perched on top. A pulley was suspended on the cable that ran between the posts. This contraption was originally called "the trolley," but by the time we were hanging on it, we just called it the zip line.

Climbing the ladder of the taller post, we crowded into the cage. With sweaty hands, one brave soul grabbed the metal handle bar that hung on the zip line. She leapt off the platform, out of the cage, and slid down to the other pole. We took turns sliding down the incline from one post to the other. Occasionally, someone slipped off and struck the ground, but it was part of the ride and why we loved it.

The zip lines are now long gone. First, the lines and handles disappeared. We still climbed up to talk over life's mysteries while we sat in the metal cages as if they were open-air forts. But eventually, even our forts were lost when the cages and posts came down, too. I'm sure it was a case of one too many broken arms and someone in charge deciding there was too much risk of serious injury.

Lighthouse Bridge is still there. I went by one afternoon and was surprised. Now that I've traveled around the country and across the globe and seen bridges from San Francisco to London, Lighthouse Bridge isn't nearly as steep as it seemed when I was riding my bike to North Palm Beach Elementary and Anchorage Park. I asked a man in a nearby neighborhood if the bridge had been lowered in a renovation. But no, the water is still twenty feet below the bottom of the bridge at high tide.

The stenciled "Walk Your Bike" sign is still there. I think my bike-riding skills might be a little rusty. Even though the bridge doesn't look as huge as it did to me in the 1960s, I may actually walk the bike now.

Anchorage Park is still there, but it doesn't look much like it did in the '60s. There are community buildings, a top-notch playground, dog parks for both small and large dogs and an improved marina. The park is designed to leave another generation of children with some great memories—even without zip lines or big swing sets.

CHAPTER 15

The Ghost of Sir Harry Oakes

The mansion looms alone on the hilltop, shrouded by huge banyan trees along U.S. Highway 1 in North Palm Beach. Saplings fight their way between cracks in the foundation. Vines climb the once proud stucco walls, and broken windows gape at the street like the vacant eyes of someone who has seen too much of the harsh side of life. Two young girls cautiously make their way up the north staircase. They hear skittering noises coming from the second floor and grab each other's hands in fear, but still, they cautiously ascend the stairs. Reaching the second-floor landing, they jump in fright as thunder booms and lightning flashes through the remains of the windows creating jagged shadows and illuminating a huge stain on the floor.

"This is where it happened," one girl says solemnly. "This is where Sir Harry Oakes was murdered!" And the lightning flashes again.

This scenario was one played out often in the minds of children growing up in North Palm Beach in the 1960s and '70s. I can say that most of the children I knew were convinced the "Oakes Mansion" was haunted. Older children made sure the younger ones had heard the much-embellished stories. Trips to the North Palm Beach Country Club involved a lot of peering at the second floor of the mansion just east of the pool to see if one could get a glimpse of Sir Harry Oakes's locally famous terrifying ghost. My cousin Tom had me convinced he had run into the ghost one cloudy afternoon as it descended the north stairs of the mansion.

The truth is that Sir Harry Oakes was in the Bahamas when he was brutally murdered in July 1943, not in North Palm Beach. His son-in-law,

Alfred de Marigny, was tried for the crime but was found innocent, and the murder remains unsolved to this day. Speculation continues among mystery buffs, and suspects include a reputed gangster as a possible culprit.

As for the "Oakes Mansion," its real name was the "Palm Beach Winter Club," and it wasn't built by Oakes. Harry Kelsey started construction in 1925 at the instigation of Paris Singer, who wanted another golf course for patrons of the hotels he had planned for his Singer Island—the luxurious Paris Singer Hotel and the Blue Heron.

Kelsey hired Louis DePuyseger, a world-renowned French architect, to design a clubhouse for the golf course he was building north of Kelsey City (now Lake Park). DePuyseger didn't disappoint. He designed a beautiful, Mediterranean-style clubhouse of three stories with "gay orange and green awnings and old Cuban tile on the roof."

Articles from the *Palm Beach Post* archives describe an incredibly elegant and sophisticated club complete with dining room. There were locker rooms in the basement and first-floor lounges. Legend has it that Al Jolson once performed an impromptu concert in the men's lounge that made him late for a scheduled performance. The third story had three bedrooms, although one article in the *Post* claimed there were twelve.

The grand opening of the Winter Club started on January 5, 1927. I say "started" because the celebration lasted three days, and guests consumed at least three boatloads of smuggled liquor. The social elite of the day gathered, and the list of attendees included the Vanderbilts, Phippses, Harrimans, Woolworths and Baches. The club opened to the public for the first time on January 9, 1927.

Charles A. Branch, hired by Harry Kelsey as a field manager in 1926, described the club in his manuscript on file with the Historical Society of Palm Beach County and the North Palm Beach Library. The early citizens of northern Palm Beach County also found other uses for the golf course.

Jules Bache, a German-born banker who was also a philanthropist and art collector, liked to take walks around the course for exercise. According to Branch, Bache spoke to him once about the plans Bache and his friends, including E.F. Hutton, had for another golf course a little farther north. That became the Seminole Club, an exclusive and world-renowned golf course to this day.

Of concern though, was the use of the golf course as a drop for smugglers. Planes flew low over the beautifully maintained grounds, and pilots threw contraband overboard to be picked up by willing accomplices on the ground. With long wilderness coastlines, Palm Beach County was ripe for smuggling, and it wasn't only criminals who participated. Even the booze served at the grand opening of the Winter Club had been smuggled in for weeks in preparation for the celebration. The local constabulary didn't always make an effort to intercede.

Shortly after the club's initial success, the 1928 hurricane season began. Palm Beach County suffered terribly in the storm that killed so many people that the actual number of victims will never be known. Mass burials were held on Tamarind Avenue in West Palm Beach because there were simply too many bodies to bury them individually. Buildings were knocked off their foundations and destroyed, several thousands of people drowned or disappeared and fortunes were lost.

The Winter Club suffered extensive damage in the 1928 hurricane and had to be temporarily closed. About this time, Harry Kelsey had some financial difficulties of his own. The Internal Revenue Service was hounding him about a debt he supposedly owed, and by the time the charges were disproved, it was too late. Kelsey, who had made his fortune with the Waldorf Restaurant chain in the Northeast, was financially ruined. His financial troubles were compounded by the hurricane. For some of the early citizens of Kelsey City, the hurricane of 1928 was a clear sign that they were meant to live somewhere else, and hundreds simply disappeared and stopped making payments on their property and were assumed to have headed back north where hurricanes were so rare they were almost nonexistent. Kelsey was forced to begin selling off property. One of the parcels of property sold included the Palm Beach Winter Club, and the buyer was Sir Harry Oakes.

Oakes was an American who became a Canadian citizen, struck it rich in the gold mines of Canada and then, in an alleged attempt to avoid Canadian taxes, became a British citizen. His story is an incredible "rags to riches" to horrible-ending story. He was knighted by King George IV in 1939 after he donated a half million dollars to St. George's Hospital in London. It is believed that Oakes bought the golf course, along with several hundred acres of property Kelsey had to sell because he wasn't welcome in the stratified Palm Beach society of the day and wanted to have a place where he was not only welcome but also hailed as the astute and successful businessman his investment accounts attested to and he believed himself to be.

Although we always knew the structure as the "Oakes Mansion," Sir Harry stayed in the clubhouse only sporadically. He managed to move some of the fairways of the golf course on the south side to accommodate his children's horses and stables—a move some said seriously impacted the beauty of the course.

After Sir Oakes's murder, the property was sold by his Tesdem Company, Inc., and eventually made its way into John D. MacArthur's portfolio and then finally to the Village of North Palm Beach.

MacArthur was one of the financial wizards of his day. His bequests of land and the parcels he sold at low prices helped create the City of Palm Beach Gardens, among others. The Village of North Palm accepted the clubhouse property eagerly and soon put it to use. The library was located there in the 1960s, and generations of children attended dance, gymnastics, art, pottery and summer camp in its aging rooms. I remember falling off the balance beam regularly in what must have been a beautiful wood-paneled office at one time and twirling to classical music in ballet lessons in what was the men's lounge.

The village built another clubhouse to the northwest and added a huge Olympic-sized pool, diving tower and restaurant. Pools weren't all that common in backyards then and the families of North Palm Beach gladly paid to be able to swim in the clear, clean water and lounge around the cement deck. When there were no little children in the baby pools, we were allowed to play in the shallow round pools next to the "Oakes Mansion." By pushing off on the bottom of the pool, we were able to get the water in the circular pools moving swiftly. When it was going fast enough, we rolled on to our backs and kept our eyes on the second floor of the aging clubhouse that loomed to the east, convinced one day, one of us would see Sir Harry.

Gradually, the clubhouse deteriorated. Bits and pieces of its history and original layout disappeared as repairs and renovations were made to make the building more usable. During a roof repair in the 1970s, the town was amazed to find two paintings that had been covered over with drywall and then forgotten in an earlier attempt to make the building more energy efficient. One of the paintings, the rectangular one, is owned by the Historical Society of Palm Beach County and is on permanent display in the Palm Beach County Governmental Center in downtown West Palm Beach.

The other painting, an oval depicting a small ship off a tropical shore, has had more interesting travels. Now hanging in the offices of the Historical Society of Palm Beach County, the ship bears the initials H.P.B.W.C.S.K, which is believed stands for "Harry—Palm—Beach—Winter—Club—Seymour—Kelsey." Painted by LeMartin Torno in 1925 for Harry Kelsey's birthday, it was later sold to Burt Reynolds, television and screen actor (who grew up in Palm Beach County). It was featured on the set of Burt Reynolds's *B.L. Stryker*, a television series that aired for the 1989–90 season. When the series folded, Reynolds donated the painting to the Loxahatchee

Don Dempsey, Sandy Dempsey (Shofner) and Diane Dempsey (Sirmans) with Palm Beach Winter Club in the background, circa 1960s. *Courtesy Dempsey family collection.*

River Historical Society. Loaned to the Historical Society of Palm Beach County for the museum's first exhibit, it's been on loan ever since. The large painting takes a minimum of four strong men to move.

The paintings weren't the only things deemed not all that important when in 1984, despite being named to the National Register of Historic Places in 1980, the Palm Beach Winter Club was demolished after huge controversy and bitter public debate. Those who fought demolition watched in tears as the remnants of the once beautiful, totally unique building was torn down. Repairs had been estimated to cost $750,000 in 1980. It had deteriorated to the point to which the village determined repairs were "too expensive" to undertake, and an empty hill now sits at 951 U.S. Highway 1.

Old concrete stairs leading to the now empty hill where the Palm Beach Winter Club was located, 2012. *Courtesy Berge family collection.*

You can, however, sit on the stone steps that once led to the clubhouse from the east. On a calm night lit by only a full moon, if you turn and look at the grassy plateau where the mansion once stood, perhaps you'll see the ghost of Sir Harry Oakes. Perhaps the ghostly forms of little ballerinas in their tutus will scamper by you on their way to a class in a building that no longer exists. Or maybe, you just might hear spectral ice tinkling in ghostly glasses as men who played a good game of golf in 1927 relax in the lounge.

CHAPTER 16

Kelsey City Gates

From Northlake Boulevard, Old Dixie Highway runs south along the west side of the railroad tracks. When I was a child, the road was two-lane asphalt and still had the feel of a country road. There were only a few buildings scattered along the road, and vacant land filled only with Florida scrub stretched out in between and behind them. The road went up and down over the slight hills—South Florida mountains!

Old Dixie was one of the original north–south routes through the area and was deliberately close to the railroad tracks. If goods weren't shipped by boat, they went by train. We traveled Old Dixie frequently on our way to the ballet lessons I took or to my mom's favorite shoe store on Park Avenue in Lake Park.

About a half block or so south of Northlake Boulevard, the main east–west thoroughfare on the border between Lake Park and North Palm Beach, we'd pass two columns of rocks, one on either side of the road. These were the remnants of the Kelsey City Gates, also known as the Kelsey City Arch. The arch as a whole was long gone by the time I rode down that street, but those remnants always drew my interest.

The story of Kelsey City started out as the story of Harry Kelsey. A visionary from Boston, he visited the area in 1919 to recover from pneumonia at his doctor's recommendation. Kelsey saw a tremendous opportunity to plan and build a city unlike any previously conceived. Kelsey sold his Waldorf Restaurants, his bakeries and his farm and, with his approximately $2.5 million ($39 million in 2010 dollars), bought as much

Harry Kelsey, founder of Kelsey City. *Courtesy Historical Society of Palm Beach County.*

land as he could, quitting only when he owned about 100,000 acres, a lot of it lakefront property. He had decided to build a resort destination in what was, at the time, barely developed ten-year-old Palm Beach County.

It was 1919 when Kelsey enlisted the Olmstead brothers, Frederick Law Jr. and John Charles, the son and adopted son of Frederick Law Olmstead, the man acknowledged as the founder of landscape architecture. The Olmstead brothers were land planners whose biggest claim to fame was the design of Central Park in New York City and the National Mall in Washington, D.C. They, along with Dr. John Nolan, designed Kelsey City, the first zoned community in the United States. The Lake Park history site states that "town plans called for three sections: residential from Lake Worth to 5th Street; retail business from 5th Street to the FEC Railroad tracks; and manufacturing and wholesale west of Dixie Highway." A large part of what they had planned is still in place today.

The nine hundred acres Kelsey set aside on the shore of Lake Worth was to include a golf resort on nearby Munyon Island, which was owned by Kelsey at the time, too.

The Kelsey Model Dairy Farm displayed the cutting edge of technology. Cows listened to classical music piped into their pristine cowsheds. The dairy farm was south of the Earman River between Alternate Route A1A and Prosperity Farms Road, land occupied by homes by the time I was riding my bike over the Earman River Bridge to tread the dirt-packed floors of the Village Store. (By the way, over the years, research has proved that Kelsey's dairymen were right: cows do produce more milk when listening to classical music.)

The little two-lane road framed by the remnants of the gate was the original U.S. Highway 1 through the area, and the gates marked the entrance to Kelsey City. Built in 1923 and measuring twenty feet high and thirty feet wide, the gates were constructed of coquina, tile, stucco and mortar wrapped around metal bars. Coquina is a soft limestone mixture of broken shells as well as corals that was commonly used in road-making and building in Florida. The arch displayed a metal banner that read, "Welcome to the World's Winter Playground." Unfortunately, the sign disappeared in the 1928 hurricane, along with the hopes and dreams of Kelsey and area residents. That hurricane changed the course of the city's development because it caused massive damage to the buildings Kelsey owned in the area as well as the fledgling town.

When U.S. Highway 1 was rerouted to the eastern location where it is today, the two-lane road next to the railroad tracks became Old Dixie Highway. In 1981, the portion of Old Dixie Highway from Northlake Boulevard south to Lake Park was slated to be enlarged to a four-lane road.

The plan was to carefully disassemble the gates and reassemble them at another location. But it didn't work out that way. When the crane touched the gates, they crumbled. Only two pieces were salvaged, and they both sit forlornly in front of the Lake Park Fire/Rescue Station on Park Avenue in

Lake Park Town Hall, 2014. *Courtesy Berge family collection.*

Lake Park. In recent years, the bronze plaques that identified the two pieces of rock and explained their importance have been stolen, but those rocks are part of what's left of the beautiful Kelsey City Gates.

Luckily, the town hall, built in 1927 and one of sixty-three buildings still standing from the initial settling of the town, remains in one piece as no one has apparently figured out how to cart it away. It was added to the National Register of Historic Places. I've attended performances in the second-floor ballroom and spent more time eyeing the beauty of the woodwork and floors than the performance.

Old Dixie may be a ghost of its former self. But for those of us who grew up traveling it, the columns for the arches are still there, and the Florida scrub still stretches to the west.

CHAPTER 17

President JFK and Peanut Island

On a sunny Florida day in 1961, my parents and I headed to the Southern Boulevard Bridge that connects Palm Beach to the mainland. I was barely two, but they brought me along to see history in person. Along with perhaps one hundred other people, we gathered at the bridge to see President John F. Kennedy as his procession traveled from the airport to the Kennedy beachfront mansion where the Kennedys had spent their winters since 1933.

As the convertible crossed the two-lane bridge, President Kennedy turned to acknowledge the onlookers perched precariously on the small sidewalks and cement railings on both sides of the structure. When his car pulled in front of my parents, the president turned in their direction and waved, seemingly right at them. Mom, frozen mid-wave, was struck into rare silence. Mom later told my father she had decided that Kennedy was one of the best-looking men she had ever seen in her life. Little black-and-white televisions and grainy newspaper pictures of the day didn't do him justice.

The procession drove on, and my mom has always remembered the day she saw those blue eyes at fifteen feet.

The world of 1961 wasn't all parades and processions for Kennedy, though. With the Cuban missile crisis less than a year away, there was already a heightened awareness in government circles concerning the country's vulnerability. Other than what Jackie Kennedy was wearing, nuclear attack was the most whispered about topic while he was in South Florida. After all, Cuba is only 283 miles away from Worth Avenue, the "main street" of the

Restored Coast Guard facility. Palm Beach Maritime Museum, Peanut Island, Florida 2012. *Courtesy Berge family collection.*

winter home for the rich and the wannabes since Flagler started developing the island in the late 1800s.

Discussions in neighborhoods all over Palm Beach County ended in debates on the pros and cons of building personal bomb shelters and bunkers in backyards. The consensus of our neighbors in North Palm Beach was that it wasn't worth building a shelter. What if it actually had to be used? How could we turn away friends and neighbors for a slight chance to save our own family? And what kind of a world would we emerge into when food ran out and we had to open the door?

But the safety of the president of the United States was a different matter. This president liked to vacation on the ocean within striking distance of nuclear missiles. As a result, in order to protect Kennedy and the stability of the U.S. government, the decision was made to build Kennedy a bomb shelter. If you've ever tried to dig a moat around a sand castle on a Florida beach, you know that digging into soil in Florida isn't easy. The water table isn't far below the surface, and the sand that makes up the barrier islands and beaches collapses too easily.

Several sites on Palm Beach were considered, but the island wasn't big enough to enable the construction of a bunker with the secrecy required. The site eventually chosen was an undeveloped island in the middle of Lake Worth. The only semi-permanent residents were men stationed at the Coast Guard facility, which had been there since 1936. The island provided light security and the possibility of easily completing a building project without too many people noticing. Operation Hotel commenced.

Originally created of mud dredged from the bottom of Lake Worth to clear the inlet for shipping, over time the island grew in size and became populated with Australian pines and not much else. Named "Peanut Island" by the locals for the peanut farm and factory that never quite got going, by the 1960s, it was a convenient spot for boaters to pause on their way home to swim, cook out or camp after a day of fishing.

The underground bomb shelter was built near the Coast Guard Station in a mound of dirt that had grown out of the refuse of previous dredging efforts. Covered with concrete and rebar, sandbags originally hid the bunker from view. It's been rumored that Kennedy visited the shelter twice—once when it was being built and once after it was completed. In a practice run, the Secret Service got him to the shelter from Palm Beach in five minutes flat. It's also been rumored that he never saw it.

When my friends and I were exploring the island in the early 1970s, the sandbags over the shelter were hidden by trees and a thick mat of pine needles. Tour guides with the Palm Beach Maritime Museum will tell you that the bomb shelter was rediscovered by boys wandering through the woods. They stumbled upon the escape hatch and, being curious, climbed down for a look. So starts many a good story, and this one was no exception. While only a couple of bunk beds and not much else were all that was left of the once well-stocked shelter, it was clear that this was not an everyday discovery.

By the time I was playing *Starsky and Hutch* in the woods a few years later, the big metal door at the entry had been cleared of debris, but it was always shut and locked. We know because we tried it every time, just in case someone forgot and it was left unlocked.

In the 1970s, Peanut Island was a rustic little island frequented only by those fortunate enough to have a boat. By 1999, development, for better or worse, had crossed the waters of Lake Worth and arrived at the island. Added fill increased the circumference of the island, and the Australian pines we loved were removed. Our beloved pines are considered an invasive plant by the Department of Agriculture because they crowd out natural Florida plants.

Today, with the restored Coast Guard station as a museum on the south side, picnic facilities, campsites, snorkeling, swimming areas manned by lifeguards and actual flushing toilets in concrete restroom buildings strategically placed around the island, it's a far cry from the Peanut Island I still see in my mind's eye. I'd hazard a guess that most of us who grew up in the paradise Florida once was would have preferred that Peanut Island remain the way longtime residents remember it.

I thought I'd hate the improvements. I'd heard that the island had become the site of a poor man's version of *Girls Gone Wild* on weekends with drinking and carousing by crazed young adults full of rum daiquiris and cheap beer. I went to see it for myself in 2012.

A friend and I decided to hitch a ride on a water taxi. While we sat waiting for the taxi at the docks, I kept looking at the shoreline of the island. It seemed way too close to the Riviera Beach Marina, and I thought it might be my memory that was faulty. But no, it was added fill. The shoreline of Peanut Island really is closer to the docks. When we arrived at the south dock in front of the Coast Guard station, my eyes popped open in surprise. We could see the door to the bunker just behind the building. Because of the pines and by design when it was built, the bunker was never visible from the water during my childhood.

We climbed the wooden steps of the boathouse, passed over the broad covered porch and bought tickets to tour the Coast Guard station and the Kennedy bunker from the Maritime Museum. While we waited for our tour guide, we wandered through the exhibits and ran with everyone else to the side of the porch when a helicopter landed on the lawn in front of the museum. Turns out there were helicopter tours of the island and, for a little extra, the island of Palm Beach, too.

The guide joined us at the back door of the boathouse and pointed out that the floors behind us were sloped so that guardsman could pull wet boats into shelter and the water would drain out of the building. The original wooden floors were still there and in good shape.

While the Coast Guard station of the Maritime Museum wasn't my focus, I still found myself fascinated. The station functioned as the only active Coast Guard facility between Fort Pierce and Miami Beach until 1995, when the Coast Guard opened a new facility on the mainland. The original station was opened to the public for tours via the Palm Beach Maritime Museum in 1999 after four years of restoration work.

We walked the short distance northwest to the bunker door. Finally, I was going to get a chance to go inside. We walked down the long metal tube that serves as an entry hall, through a decontamination shower, and into the bunker. It was large and airy considering it was a hole in the ground. The presidential seal was painted on the floor by the museum, and it was an impressive sight. A desk sat behind the seal with an American flag on a pole. It was possible to imagine Kennedy sitting there attempting to guide the country through nuclear war, even though, fortunately, he never faced that horrendous situation and the bunker never looked like that during his lifetime.

Cans of fresh water and an unused barrel system for human waste were displayed. Two bunk beds sat against the walls and were covered with framed newspaper clippings about Kennedy and his time in Palm Beach. Several of the pictures and news articles concerned Marilyn Monroe. (I still can't figure out what she had to do with the shelter, though.) On the back wall was the escape hatch the boys had first climbed down to rediscover the shelter. Looking up, I could see the hatch door outlined in the bright Florida sunshine. I really hope there was a better seal in the 1960s.

The tour guide explained that because the bunker was twenty-five feet underground, it had been prone to flooding in high tides. What would have

Author in front of the Kennedy Bunker entrance. Palm Beach Maritime Museum, Peanut Island, Florida, 2012. *Courtesy Berge family collection. Photograph by Becky Young.*

happened if it had flooded after a nuclear disaster with the president of the United States seeking shelter isn't clear. I suppose it was never expected to be a long-term solution. After years of flooding, the bunker was in sad shape when it was first accessed again by those curious boys. None of the original furniture survived in usable condition.

While Peanut Island is nothing like I remember, I can't say the development was all bad. It's beautiful, albeit different, and the people working there are friendly and knowledgeable as to the history of the island and the buildings. As my friend and I sat on the big porch at the Coast Guard boathouse, it felt like a mini-vacation somewhere other than fifteen minutes away from home.

If you enjoy a bit of history, take the Palm Beach Maritime Museum tour. As you stand on the cement sidewalk in front of that door waiting your turn to walk into history, try to picture the imposing metal door surrounded not by small trees and neatly trimmed shrubs but buried under pine needles and framed by tall gently whispering Australian pines. Next to you, a small, skinny blonde girl with big blue eyes and eyebrows knitted in concentration tries to imagine what's behind that big heavy door.

Tell her she'll be able to see for herself in about forty years.

CHAPTER 18

The Involuntary Cowherd

I have to admit that I really don't remember who the child in the hall was and have taken literary license to tell this story.

I rode my bike to Allamanda Elementary for sixth grade in 1971 even though I had spent most of the previous years at North Palm Beach Elementary. It was the era of enforced busing, and the school boundaries had changed. My entire neighborhood was reassigned from North Palm Beach Elementary to Allamanda.

As sixth graders, we ruled the school. I was on the safety patrol and wore a bright orange patrol belt and badge from the American Automobile Association. We put the flag up at the beginning of the school day and brought it down at the end. We were the responsible kids—the helpers. We were the ones who looked out for younger kids and took pride in doing so. I moved up the ranks until I became captain, and it was my job to assign posts for all of the patrol officers.

Our neighborhood was too close to ride the bus to our new elementary school, so we rode our bikes. This was nothing new; we hadn't been able to ride the bus to North Palm Beach Elementary, either. The ride to North Palm involved going east and over the Lighthouse Bridge.

Our new route was a trek across Lighthouse Drive, the main east–west road through the village, past Lighthouse Baptist Church, the baseball fields and behind St. Claire's Catholic Church, over a little wooden footbridge crossing a usually dry gully, over a paved path that wound between fences

Florida commissioner of agriculture Nathan Mayo with Elsie, the Borden cow. *State Archives of Florida, Florida Memory, http://floridamemory.com/items/show/136964.*

through cow pastures and into the school bike parking lot. Just shy of three miles, it took us fifteen to twenty minutes to transverse, depending on how long we dawdled on the way.

The absolute best safety patrol post was the one on the bridge. Patrol members on duty would park their bikes beside the path and make all the younger kids get off their bikes and then walk them across the ten-foot bridge like it was really, really dangerous. While waiting for more bicyclists to get to the bridge, the patrol officer on duty stood by the small bridge in the middle of the fields and enjoyed the morning.

In hindsight, I suppose the cows could have been more dangerous than the bridge. If they ever had decided to rush the fence and bike path in a mad stampede, we'd have been trampled for sure. Of course, these were Florida cows, and they were usually so sapped of energy by the heat they just stood there and ignored us. And like cows everywhere, they were not good at organizing.

When I was the student with the orange sash on duty at the footbridge, time often stretched between bike riders, and I grew bored of standing there, leaning on the railing. I'd moo at a nearby cow to see if I could get a reaction. The most I ever got was a turned head and a bored, bovine stare. Occasionally, a moo would come in the distance as if to remind me they were out there—watching and waiting.

There was a long history of cattle ranching in Florida. Cows had been part of the economy in Florida long before I arrived in 1959.

Spaniards first brought cattle from Spain and Cuba to support the garrison of St. Augustine in 1565. Cattle had become so important by the 1700s that the Seminole Indian chief during that time bore the name "Cowkeeper." Cows escaped and flourished in the wild, and the legend of the Florida "cracker cow hunter" was born. Because the land was so wild and expansive, it took hunters several days to track down cows that escaped their herds and ran off into the Florida scrub. By the late 1960s, most cattle were in registered herds, and only a few of the original wild cracker cattle stock were left.

In my childhood, there were pastures all over Palm Beach County where cows grazed in contentment. Of course, that also might have had something to do with the property appraiser and real estate taxes. If you had a few cows grazing on vacant land, the land was considered agricultural property, and taxes on that land would be much lower than the taxes on residential or commercial property.

Near the end of my sixth-grade year at Allamanda, one of the cows apparently decided that she was different from all the other cows in the pasture. She was going to take a stroll on the wild side. I was en route from my classroom to the office with the attendance report in my hand when I stopped dead in my tracks just outside the door. At the end of the hallway, a large cow blocked the way.

Why was she there? I had no idea. Maybe she had a beef about the way things were run out in the field. Maybe someone had let the grass grow too tall out there until it was past her eyes. Or perhaps she was just in the mooed to see what the inside of a school looked like. OK, OK. I'm through milking the puns.

Kid and cow eyed each other. The smell of fresh grass from the fields wafted off her huge brown and white hide. Her hooves looked much bigger than they appeared when she was standing in the pasture. Her big, glassy eyes fixed on me one at a time as she turned her head from one side to the other, all the while chewing her cud. I tried to calculate whether I could safely run past her to the office or whether I should just make a hasty retreat. The cow was apparently making a similar calculation—that is, whether there was anything worth eating on me or in my hand. Perhaps that wasn't grass the cow was chewing.

After a stare down that lasted several seconds, my mind raced as I tried to figure out the best course of action. Inching backward toward the classroom, I fixed my eyes on the cow. She took a few tentative steps down the hall toward me. I turned and ran the last few steps into the class, slamming the door behind me. Twenty-three heads snapped up to look at me. The captain of the safety patrols was the last one anyone expected to break the rules by running through the hall or slamming a door.

"Cow!" I yelled.

Every student, and the teacher, looked at me like I had escaped from the state mental hospital in Chattahootchee. Not that any of us had ever been in or near Chattahootchee, but most of our parents had complained we belonged there at one time or another.

"There's a cow in the hall!" I shouted, and I was shoved aside as all the students ran to the door.

Mrs. Paul, the teacher, attempted to take control of the situation and yelled, "Wait! Wait! Children! Move back!"

We tried to peer at the cow that kept ambling slowly but surely down the hall toward our classroom door.

The teacher finally managed to pull us all back in the room by pointing out that if we left the door open, the cow would come in the classroom. None of us thought this was a good idea.

She called the principal on the intercom. "Mr. Powell? Mr. Powell?"

"Yes," came the reply.

"Sir, there's a cow in the sixth grade hallway."

There was a few seconds of static from the speaker on the wall followed by, "Would you repeat that, Mrs. Paul?"

"I said there's a cow. A cow is in the hall." She spoke each word slowly, loudly and distinctly.

We all turned toward the speaker waiting for instructions on what to do next, but there was only static.

"Mr. Powell?"

Within two minutes, Mr. Powell, a middle-aged man wearing black horn-rimmed glasses, who was possibly wondering just when cow herding had been added to his job description, appeared at the end of the hall. He stopped abruptly and, hands on hips, slowly shook his head back and forth.

We heard him say, "Shoo" as he flapped his arms and bravely herded the cow out the end of the hall and back behind the pasture fencing.

My classmates and I were impressed. The tale became part of the school's legend. Mr. Powell was hailed as the hero who saved the entire sixth grade from the killer cow.

Years later, when my brother attended the same school, the legend had faded into history. Very few students knew the story, and only a few of the teachers had stayed the seven years between me and my brother. I would bet, though, that there are more than a few men and women around my age who remember that cow and the legend of Mr. Powell, the involuntary cowherd.

CHAPTER 19

The Spectacular Christmas in Dixie Parade

Even though the Lake Park Historical Society has pictures of a "Christmas in Dixie" parade held in the 1920s, the first modern parade by that name was organized in 1954 in Riviera Beach by Jerry Kelly. Usually held on a Sunday early in December, the Christmas in Dixie parade was an institution in northern Palm Beach County from 1954 until the early 1990s. I don't remember that there were any other parades quite as large. The climax of the parade was the float at the end with a plump, bearded, smiling Santa Claus. It signaled the beginning of the Christmas season to generations of kids, including me.

In the December 15, 1969 edition, the *Palm Beach Post* referred to the Christmas in Dixie parade as the "Biggest Florida parade outside of the Orange Bowl spectacle." The Orange Bowl was in Miami and was televised. In that parade, girls in bathing suits on professionally built floats waved to spectators under streetlights. My brother and I were parade junkies and cried until our parents let us stay up late to watch the Orange Bowl parade on TV. We were way too young and not nearly cynical enough to realize that a large reason the Orange Bowl parade existed was as advertising to lure Yankees to the warmth of Florida during tourist season. "Look at us!" the parade yelled. "You're up there in the snow and ice, and we're in bathing suits under palm trees!"

That year, our Christmas in Dixie parade included the Miami Mummer's Band in addition to the floats, fire engines, bands and clowns. It may not have been on television other than a quick clip on the local news, but we

Float, 1970s. *Photograph by Harry Wright.*

sat awe-struck on the curbs and danced in excitement as if it were televised to the nation. Those were the days when future actors and actresses were discovered in soda shops, so it was entirely possible that a Hollywood producer could see a spectator at a parade and make her a star.

My family would settle in for the wait along the route, which, until police closed the barricades, still had traffic. Young occupants of the back seats of passing cars pointed toward empty spaces on one side or the other, trying to get their parents to pull over immediately. The smell of coconuts mixed with hot asphalt was everywhere as we, and everyone around us, had thoroughly doused ourselves and one another with sunscreen. In Florida, despite the calendar saying December, it was often hot and sunny. When cars trickled to a stop, my brother would dash into the four-lane street, along with a gaggle of other little boys, waiting for a glimpse of the military color guard proudly holding the American and state of Florida flags that heralded the start of the parade.

When we heard the faint music in the distance that marked the parade's impending arrival, everyone stood and elbowed his or her way to the front. We craned our necks around and over one another in order to be first to see the American flag. We tried hard to catch a glimpse without stepping more than a foot or two into the street to avoid parental wrath. When the flag appeared down the street in the hands of the uniformed color guard—the local high school Reserve Officer Training Corps or the Veterans of Foreign Wars—everyone lining the parade route stood quietly, hand over heart in respect. Dads' hands smacked anyone under age ten who wouldn't stand still or dared to speak.

"That's the American flag. You better hush up and stand in respect or else!" my dad or another one nearby threatened.

We did our part as spectators. We waved furiously at the kids on the floats and anyone in the parade who looked our way. We stood and danced when the marching bands came by, and we oohed and aahed where it was expected. We bought souvenirs from the vendors who walked up and down the street selling cotton candy and other things we tried desperately to convince our parents were necessary to life.

Girl Scouts, Boy Scouts and Indian Guides marched in uniform, waving first at the spectators on one side of the street and then on the other. One year, a mom got the idea that it would be cute to have her Girl Scout troop dress up as presents. The "presents" marched in cardboard boxes from the grocery store wrapped in Christmas paper with holes cut out for their heads and arms. Huge bows and tags completed the ensemble. It looked like someone's idea of a nightmare in which Christmas presents came to life and ran amok down the street on legs clad in candy cane tights. By the time they passed our lawn chairs, bows drooped, Shirley Temple curls hung limply, makeup streaked down red cheeks and the energetic waves to the crowd of spectators from the beginning of parade route were merely weak flapping of fingers out of the gaping holes in the sides of the boxes.

There was always at least one group of tumbling gymnasts. I envied their skill and felt sorry for them, even though their hands were in gloves, as they did cartwheels and handsprings along the entire parade route.

Church groups spent weeks building elaborate nativities on flatbed trailers. Shimmering tinsel garlands were festooned down the sides. The local hardware stores were cleaned out of chicken wire and two by fours to build float structures. Prior to the parade, hordes of volunteers would scrunch different colors of tissue paper in the metal gaps to create designs. More ambitious float builders had real palm trees draped in tinsel and dotted with Christmas ornaments anchored to the flatbed surface in plastic pots. The children of each church rode, clinging on for dear life, while they sang Christmas carols at the top of their lungs. They had to practically scream in order to be heard. For some unknown reason, these floats were always positioned in front or behind one of the high school

Indian Guides in front of Lake Park Town Hall, possibly 1970. *Courtesy Hartman family collection. Photograph by Margaret Hartman.*

bands. A lot of them had teenagers with gray wigs and costumes to look like Mrs. Claus or the three wise men. A crowd favorite was Mary, Joseph and baby Jesus. It was more entertaining if the babe was screaming while Joseph, fake beard firmly affixed to his hairless cheeks with spirit gum, that sticky glue used by theatrical productions everywhere to remedy a lack of chin hair, and Mary, with her long straight hair and braces on her teeth, tried their teenage best to calm him.

Near the end of the parade was a float for the local Junior Orange Bowl princesses. These girls from each town had won the local pageant and would be going to Miami for the statewide pageant to try to win the coveted position as Junior Orange Bowl Queen. That prize came with a ride on a big float in the Junior Orange Bowl Parade in Miami and a shot at stardom as you'd just *have* to be discovered when you rode on a float in *that* parade.

Miss Christmas in Dixie and her court had their own float, too. Float-riders were required to wave regally when they weren't tossing candy to kids. By the time they reached the end, there weren't many Christmas sweets left. Arms ached, and Christmas cheer was in short supply.

As much fun as the parade was to watch, if you had an older cousin or sibling in one of the high school bands, you were really a big shot. In our world, you reached the pinnacle of success only if you actually marched or rode on a float in the parade.

My friend Kelly took baton-twirling lessons and joined the troops of budding majorettes who marched down the street in their matching brightly colored leotards and tights. In one Christmas parade, somewhere south of Northlake Boulevard, Kelly's baton made a suicidal leap out of her hand and rolled into the only drainage opening in the curb for fifty yards in either direction. She ran after the baton, knelt in the gravel and dirt of the street and stuck her arm in after it, but it was hopeless. The baton had disappeared into the water drainage system. She rocked back on her heels for a moment and pondered what to do. When her friends started calling her, she ran back to her group and with dirty knees and torn tights, twirled an imaginary baton the rest of the parade. None of the parade spectators noticed she was just moving her hand around, but she was grounded for losing it when the parade was over and her mother asked why she no longer had the baton.

Music has always been important in our family, and it was a big part of the spectacular Christmas in Dixie parade. My brother, John, who is six years younger than me, marched with the North Shore High School marching band during his years in high school. I came home from college to applaud from the sidelines. The band marched with quick steps in precise formation down the street and stopped just past us. Then they started gyrating to a drumbeat. The band director had been a member of the FAMU ("Florida Agricultural and Mechanical University") band in Tallahassee. They were well known for their dancing and high stepping as well as their playing. It may have been all the rage in college marching bands in the 1970s, but my dad—a musician since high school, when he had played a tuba and was drilled in Sousa marches—was horrified. That year, we heard all the way home that no marching band should play anything but Sousa marches and something must be wrong with that band director to let those kids dance like that. My brother and I kept silent. We thought the dancing was cool.

The last entry in the parade was always Santa Claus. When kids saw Santa and his reindeer mysteriously hovering in the air coming down the street, ecstasy and pandemonium erupted. It meant that it was finally, officially, Christmas season. There were only a few more weeks that they would have to keep trying to be good to avoid the stocking filled with coal.

Santa's elves, coincidentally dressed in the same candy cane tights the Girl Scout Christmas packages wore, walked on either side of Santa's float and tossed candy to the kids who dashed to collect peppermints and gum balls while parents started packing up for the long hike back to the car. Behind Santa's float, the real world came back, and people who had finished watching the parade were lined up in their cars to patiently follow

Santa's float across town. Kids riding along waved at the spectators from their parents' station wagons as if they were riding a float instead of stuck in an avocado-colored panel wagon.

In the mid-1980s, scandal erupted when Bob Plimpton, the organizer that year, had the audacity to put young women in bikinis on the floats. The town was stunned and outraged. Of course, by then the Orange Bowl had been doing it in the Sodom and Gomorrah that was Miami, and the French (oh, the French!) had been wearing bikinis for forty years. Even Bridgette Bardot had been prancing around in one since 1957. After much yelling and many horrified letters to the editors in all the local newspapers, a compromise was reached. Bathing suits were allowed, and the parade went on for another few years.

On December 13, 1992, the much-loved Christmas in Dixie parade met its sad end. In a fit of jealousy over a boy, a fifteen-year-old girl near the end of the parade route, in a dramatic example of young love out of control, threw a bottle at her fourteen-year-old rival marching in the parade with the Jingling Babies, a dance team. During the riot that followed, the Jingling Babies, swinging fake candy canes like baseball bats, were joined by an estimated one thousand people. Four people were arrested, and two police officers were injured. It took police from five different jurisdictions to stop the free for all. After more than thirty years, more if the parade in the '20s is counted, a cherished small-town tradition disappeared.

CHAPTER 20

Singer Island Dreams

Off the coast of Palm Beach County, just north of the Lake Worth Inlet, lies a small, lush barrier island called Singer Island.

We often crossed the Blue Heron Bridge to go to the public beaches along the ocean or to "Mother's Beach" on the little spit of land where the bridge touched down two-thirds of the way across Lake Worth. Also known as Causeway Beach, the bit of beach was part of Phil Foster Park, named in 1953 after one of the earliest settlers of Riviera Beach. The beach facing the inlet was called Mother's Beach because waves were tame there compared to waves on the ocean. On that tiny sand beach, mothers were able to keep a more relaxed eye on swimming children.

When I was growing up, mom-and-pop motels and vacation apartments dotted the southern end of the island with the impressive and imposing Colonnades Beach Hotel towering over the neighborhood. To the north was Air Force Beach, the local nude beach beloved by area fishermen who conveniently had to pass by on their way to and from their favorite fishing spots. To locals, it will always be Air Force Beach, the name it picked up when servicemen stationed in Palm Beach County frequented the sand and reefs there. These days, however, the area is formally known as John D. MacArthur Beach State Park. (For more on Air Force Beach, see Chapter 22, Sun, Sand and a Lot of Skin.)

One year, Dad was unable to leave his business for a summer vacation, and it was decided that Mom, my brother and I would spend the week at the Holiday Inn next to the public beach on Singer Island. We played on the beach during the day, and Dad joined us for dinner. Not much fun for him, but looking back, I think it was fortunate we lived in paradise and were able to vacation a few minutes from home.

Paris Singer of Palm Beach, circa 1900s. *State Archives of Florida, Florida Memory, http://floridamemory.com/items/show/153286.*

The Colonnades hosted *Treasure Isle*, a short-lived television program (1967–68) that featured couples rowing through man-made water features and digging up prize cards with pictures of what they had just won. The host during the brief run on ABC was John Bartholomew Tucker, who later was cohost of *The New Candid Camera* in 1974. I heard a rumor that on occasion, local smart alecks would creep onto the open set the night before filming and dig up the prize cards. Did TV producers really bury prizes the night before taping? Perhaps not, but one wonders what would have happened the next day when contestants raced to a little sand island to find no prize, only sand.

Across from the public beach was an old hotel with a strip club on the first floor. It was owned by parents of a friend of mine, and my friend and I occasionally accompanied one of her parents there during the day when they needed to catch up on office work. Often, we sat at the bar in our eleven-year-old glory enjoying a soda. We thought we were very grown up. And no, the bar wasn't open, and there was no entertainment provided other than the fun we had running around the empty booths and pretending to be famous singers on the small stage.

As teenagers, my friends and I practically lived at the beach when we weren't working or in school. The long walk across bright white burning sand to get to the surf led to steam around our feet by the time we got to the water. Well, not really, but until we developed the "towel-sand hop," our feet bore the brunt of the heat. The towel-sand hop involved tossing a towel on the sand in front of one, hopping onto it, tossing another towel farther out and hopping to that towel. It took a while to get to the surf that way, but the hop resulted in far less pain for the feet. Eventually, a boardwalk was built on the south end of the beach that you could take most of the way toward the ocean, reducing the towel-sand hop to a mere twenty or so yards.

After lying on the sand and soaking in the ocean water for hours, we trudged up to the old shops that lined the road along the public beach to buy a candy necklace and a soda. The taste of the hard candy beads threaded with elastic that we wore around our necks is hard to describe. The sweetness of the candy combined with salt from the ocean and coconut from our suntan lotion created a unique taste. We still ate every piece—never fast enough to avoid a multicolored tattoo around our necks, though. For lunch, we walked even farther and consumed sandwiches at the Grater Gator on the other side of the public parking lot.

Singer Island was originally the northern part of the island of Palm Beach. The ocean is to the east and the then freshwater Lake Worth to the west. The northern and southern parts of the island were separated when the inlet was carved from the ocean to Lake Worth to allow ships to enter what became the Port of Palm Beach. The inlet was further dredged by the federal government in 1918, and the fill created nearby Hood's Island (now Peanut Island). It became the home of "Inlet City" around 1906. Home primarily to fishermen and their families, as well as squatters, men with wives and children gravitated to the north and single men to the south. Inlet City was small with only one store and a church that served as the school on weekdays.

Paris Eugene Singer, the twenty-third and last child of Isaac Singer, bought the island in bits and pieces with his inherited wealth. The Singer family made its fortune in the design and sale of Singer sewing machines. Paris, like his father, Isaac, led a very interesting life that included an affair with famed dancer Isadora Duncan, with whom he had an illegitimate son.

Having already built the Everglades Club farther south on the island of Palm Beach, Singer looked a little farther north. It was April 1918 when the *Palm Beach Post* reported that after making a half dozen purchases prior to April, Singer bought the Hammon property from City Builders Realty Company. In February 1925, Singer bought the Huston tract from Anderson T. Herd in the biggest land deal to date. He paid $2 million. Herd had just bought the property two weeks prior and, with the sale to Singer, made a huge profit. In June 1925, Singer paid $1.5 million for the "Blue Heron" tract of 5,200 feet from George Fryhofer and Edward E. Jenkins. The total in purchases is estimated to be the stunning sum of $4 million. (In 2012, that would be $47 million.)

Singer had huge dreams for what was then known as "Singer's Island," later shortened by the locals to "Singer Island." He intended to build two luxury hotels, the Paris Singer Hotel on the south side and the Blue Heron to the north, with a golf course between the two. Singer was going to finance the building of the hotels by the sale of lots and lined up Addison Mizner, a well-known architect later revered as the mastermind of the "Palm Beach" look, as his architect. Singer and Mizner agreed on a retainer of $6,000 per year for life to restrict Mizner's grand designs to the Palm Beach area.

Singer wanted high-rise bridges to connect the island to the mainland and even considered a tunnel under the inlet. Government officials weren't interested in the tunnel, but in 1925, the local government built a wooden bridge called "Sherman's Point Bridge" from the mainland to the area near the Blue Heron building site at Sherman's Point. Singer had also convinced Harry Kelsey—founder of Kelsey City and a landowner with huge holdings in the northern area of the county—to build the Palm Beach Winter Club to service his future guests.

Unfortunately, only the service wing of the Blue Heron was built before the hurricane of 1928 surged through the area. Most buildings in the path of that horrendous storm were either destroyed or damaged severely. The fledgling hotel was no exception and was irreparable. Sherman's Point Bridge was also damaged and had to be replaced. In the financial devastation, fear of future storms and the stock market crash that followed, lots remained unsold. Singer abandoned his dreams and left the area. He died in London in 1932.

Singer Island retained Paris Singer's name even as it sat deserted except for fishermen and the local teenagers who hung out at the beach until the 1940s. Then the City of Riviera Beach bought beachfront property on the east side of the island. A.O. Edwards, a British builder of railroads in England, India and South Africa, purchased an additional 240 acres in 1947. Edwards, who also renovated the Savoy Hotel in London and built the Mayfair and Grosvenor Hotels in 1927, developed the southern end of the island into the town of Palm Beach Shores, which looks today very much like it did when it was first developed. The walkways, parks and roads are in their original locations.

We had Girl Scout meetings in the community center, and one of the biggest treats after a meeting was to follow the nine-block walkway lined with palms and tropical plants from the community center to the inlet, where we watched boats navigate in and out of Lake Worth.

In 1948, Edwards built the Inlet Court Motel. After his death in 1960, it was purchased by local magnate and land developer John D. MacArthur.

Above: Palm Beach Shores Town Hall. Palm Beach Shores, Florida, 2014. *Courtesy Berge family collection.*

Left: Pathway to Inlet Park from Palm Beach Shores Town Hall. Palm Beach Shores, Florida, 2014. *Courtesy Berge family collection.*

Singer Island Public Beach, 2014. *Courtesy Berge family collection.*

Renaming the motel the Colonnades Beach Hotel, MacArthur conducted business in the bar there as he became the largest landowner in the area, eventually donating the land on the north side of the island now known as John D. MacArthur Beach State Park to the state of Florida. MacArthur bought land that had been owned by Harry Kelsey and later Sir Harry Oakes. This land later became North Palm Beach and Palm Beach Gardens.

The Colonnades Beach Hotel is gone. The building was demolished in 1990, and Marriott's Ocean Pointe was built on the land. The Marriott sits at the southern end of Singer Island, nestled between the small apartments of Palm Beach Shores and the ocean, just as the Colonnades did. The public beach is still there, too, although long gone are the candy necklaces and the tiny shop that carried them. Luckily, the Grater Gator is still across the public parking lot, where it's been sitting since at least 1963.

The bridge connecting the island to the mainland was rebuilt in 1976, and although the official name is the Jerry Thomas Memorial Bridge, to locals, the bridge is known by the name of Singer's dream hotel of long ago, the Blue Heron.

CHAPTER 21

The Six Mackerel Day

My dad was a fisherman. Oh, he didn't fish for a living, but he was one of those guys who grew up with salt water in his veins. I don't think he ever spent enough time far enough away from a coast that he missed the smell of the salt air. In our collection of family photos is one of my dad and his brother Warren, who was roughly a year younger. The two skinny boys, dressed like Huck Finn and Tom Sawyer, are standing proudly in front of their handmade boat, ready to go fishing.

When early settlers made their way to the eastern coast of what is now Palm Beach County, they were delighted to find a freshwater lake where fish were plentiful and the water was pristine. It didn't stay that way long, though. One of the stories says that a deserter from the Confederate army showed up in the area early on and proceeded to dig a canal with a conch shell from the lake to the ocean nearby to create Lake Worth Inlet. That's probably not quite true, though. The low-lying land between the pump house on Singer Island to the north and Worth Avenue on Palm Beach to the south frequently flooded, and the water would create a channel. Sometimes, the water was high enough that boats could sail through, but just as often, the channel wasn't passable. In 1887, a group of early settlers literally took matters into their own hands and helped the cause by digging farther north from the current location. After initial success, that channel shifted south to where it is now. The end result—whether it was the romantic notion that a single man started it all or not—was that the brackish seawater was invited inland, and by 1915, a dredged channel existed. In 1925, the Lake Worth

Author and brother boating in the Lake Worth, 1969. *Courtesy Hartman family collection.*

Inlet District and area leaders decided that if another inlet was created at the south end of the lake, it might help the circulation of the water and take away some of the pollution. Thus, South Lake Worth Inlet was created. It's also known as Boynton Inlet.

Often on a Saturday morning in the 1970s, Mom loaded an ice chest with picnic and grilling supplies. Half asleep, we helped Dad stuff everything in the paneled station wagon. As we drove through North Palm Beach, there were few other cars on the road. As we crossed Lighthouse Bridge, there were no bike riders.

At the marina, provisions were unloaded and carried to the boat, where they were stowed for later. Dad double-checked everything, stem to stern, and we were ready to go. As we headed south from the North Palm Beach Marina toward the widest part of Lake Worth, I clambered to my favorite spot at the prow of the boat and sat, hanging my feet over as we pulled out of the boat slip and headed to the lake. I loved to lean my forearms on the railing and had a little rhyme I worked on in my head every time we were on the water: "When the water is colored like elephant skin, it protects all that hides within." I never got past that first line, but I liked it and chanted it to the rhythm of the boat slapping the small inland waves. Fifteen minutes later, we passed the Blue Heron Bridge that connected the mainland to Singer Island. (See Chapter 20 for more about Paris Singer and his development dreams for the island.)

The boat bobbed as Dad aimed the bow toward the ocean. He liked to troll for fish, although he seldom took us out of the inlet with him. The waves caused the boat to bump and jar us all as we made our way out to the smoother waters of the wide-open sea. Once we were far enough out, Dad put the two inboard-outboard motors in idle, and we helped bait and throw lines off the back of the boat. He concentrated on where the boat was heading, and we watched the lines as they fed into the water behind the boat. If we saw a slight dip of the fishing rod, we hollered to Dad, who wrestled the fish into the boat.

Lake Worth Inlet facing east toward the ocean, 2014. The island of Palm Beach is to the right. *Courtesy Berge family collection.*

Lake Worth Inlet from the southern edge of Singer Island, 2014. The island of Palm Beach is to the left. The Port of Palm Beach is straight ahead. *Courtesy Berge family collection.*

One Saturday, we hadn't caught many fish in the ocean, and Dad decided that we would fish Lake Worth itself. When we were safely back inside the inlet, Dad anchored the boat, and we baited and threw lines out. My rod dipped immediately, and Dad helped me pull in a mackerel. The fish was tossed into a cooler, and the line was baited and tossed again. Again, my fishing rod dipped almost as soon as the bait hit the water. Another mackerel! The second went into the cooler with the first. Fish after fish appeared to fight one another for the privilege of jumping on my hook. I quickly caught six fish on one rapidly deteriorating fly. After the last fish, Dad clipped the now straggly looking fly off the line and handed it to me. It was my souvenir from the day I caught six mackerel on one hook and had impressed the lifelong fisherman in my life with my fishing prowess.

CHAPTER 22

How Floridians Stand the Heat

It's hot and sticky outside. Then again, it is every summer. Other than sitting inside in the air conditioning, where can a Floridian go to escape the heat and humidity?

On Military Trail south of Blue Heron Boulevard lies the perfect place to be on a hot summer day in Florida. The Rapids has everything from sedate children's sections (Tadpool and Splish Splash Lagoon) to Big Thunder with its forty-five-degree drop and speeds of up to twenty miles per hour.

The Rapids has been around a long time. I was thirteen or so when my family went camping in the campground now tucked behind the huge Rapids Water Park. In 1979, the owner of the campground thought water slides might be a nice amenity to offer his campers. He built a hill and installed four flumes on four acres of land. We rode those four flumes over and over and begged to stay the entire day so we could ride them more.

The owner decided campers weren't the only people who might enjoy cooling off on a water slide, so he opened it to everyone who could come up with the small admission fee. Today, those original flumes are still in the park. Called Old Yellar, they're tame compared to rides like Black Thunder, Big Thunder and Tubin' Tornadoes.

It was 2012 when I slipped on a bathing suit and a pair of shorts, slapped a ball cap on my head, packed my sunscreen and headed over to the Rapids again. I walked through the entire park, a feat in itself because the park is now thirty acres. As I walked, I heard the screams of terror and joy as children and adults braved the waters. Everywhere I looked, people were

Original four slides still in use at the Rapids. Riviera Beach, 2012. *Courtesy Berge family collection.*

smiling. I rode around the Lazy River a couple of times in an inner tube. There were no fish swimming beneath me as there would be in a natural spring, but around a corner, an unexpected fountain of water thoroughly soaks those floating by.

I rode the waves in the wave pool and relaxed in my lounge chair under a huge shade tree next to the Lazy River. I decided to stay for a while and sat peacefully and watched the park slow down as closing time approached. As shadows lengthened, I became aware that the sound of rushing water had stopped. Fountains were turned off, and fewer inner tubes, now all sans passengers, drifted by my chair. The lifeguards (Red Cross certified) pulled tubes out of the water and straightened the chairs around me.

I asked a couple of lifeguards what they liked most about working at the Rapids. Dan, who's been working at the Rapids for four years, told me that he liked being outside. He said his job is fun, and he enjoys meeting people. He also enjoys the rides when he's not working. Katie is a first-year lifeguard at the park. She just moved down from New York and enjoys watching guests smile. She likes being able to help them.

Lazy River at the Rapids. Riviera Beach, 2012. *Courtesy Berge family collection.*

It's a good thing the two enjoy people and a great thing that the park grew from just those four flumes because somewhere in the neighborhood of 400,000 people visit each year.

And the water is just as cold as it was in the 1970s.

CHAPTER 23

Sun, Sand and a Lot of Skin

A nude beach? In Palm Beach County? Well, yes, there was. It wasn't very big, but rumor has it that as many as three thousand sun worshipers sometimes bathed au naturel on the sand there on any given weekend.

Air Force Beach, as it was known then, was beloved by quite a few in northern Palm Beach County, and not all were sunbathers. According to Deborah Murray of the Historical Society of Palm Beach County, "Air Force Beach became the U.S. Air Force Beach when Morrison Field was reactivated during the Korean War. The Air Force had to have its own beach as the beaches were segregated then and they needed a beach where both blacks and whites could congregate. It was not U.S. Army Air Corps property during World War II." The Korean War started in 1950 and ended in 1953.

The nudity went on a bit longer, though, and I know we were calling the area Air Force Beach in the 1970s. Natives of the area still do. Local historian Eliot Kleinberg posted on www.historicpalmbeach.com that the nude beach was active into the 1980s. I remember my dad coming home from a full day of fishing complaining that his fishing buddy, Cecil, insisted on sailing really, really, really slowly past Air Force Beach, binoculars in hand. As a child, I didn't see why that was such a problem, and no one would explain it.

If you'd like to partake of the nude sunbathing, don't bother running down to Air Force Beach these days. The land was bought by John D. MacArthur, who donated it to the State of Florida in the 1970s for the creation of John D. MacArthur Beach State Park. Mr. MacArthur enjoyed communing with nature himself and reportedly once invited Walt Disney to join him there

MacArthur State Park, aka Air Force Beach, 2014. *Courtesy of Land & Sea Imagery. Photograph by Fred Holmstock.*

MacArthur State Park, aka Air Force Beach, 2014. *Courtesy of Land & Sea Imagery. Photograph by Fred Holmstock.*

in the 1960s when MacArthur was trying to entice Disney to build his next theme park in Palm Beach County. Holy Mickey Mouse! Whether the rumor is true or not, I'll never watch reruns of *The Wonderful World of Walt Disney* quite the same way again.

The state park opened to the public in 1989, about seven years after the State of Florida declined to continue protecting the nude beach. Guides there can take you on kayak tours of prehistoric Indian middens (a mound of shells and assorted other things that indicate humans were once living there) and point out the ruins of Dr. James Munyon's epic Hygeia Hotel on Munyon Island. (The hotel burned to the ground in 1915. The tale of Dr. Munyon is in Chapter 28, Where the Pawpaw Grew. Con man or genius? It's still up for debate.)

John D. MacArthur Beach State Park is a beautiful and unusual park that provides nesting grounds for rare turtles and beautiful endangered birds and has a reef right off the shore accessible for snorkelers who don't have boats.

Visitors should be aware of the wildlife, though. On a visit there in the late 1990s, I stood on the beach watching in awe as bull sharks and tarpon herded baitfish toward the shore for a meal. Of course, I didn't have a camera. The tarpon were leaping in the air over the baitfish. It was incredible. I ended up arguing with a tourist who thought it was quite all right to stand in the middle of the swarming baitfish with her daughter next to her and baby granddaughter in her arms. Her argument? "Oh, they don't want to eat ME. They want to eat the little fish!" It took me yelling at her that sharks aren't known for their eyesight and one could easily take a bite out of her by mistake before she finally stepped out of the water onto the safety of the sand.

Located at the northern tip of Singer Island, it's worth the trip even if you have to wear a bathing suit.

CHAPTER 24

Sunshine and Dark Shadows

When I heard Hollywood was making a movie out of the classic television series *Dark Shadows* in 2012, I was thrilled. I was less than thrilled when I heard it was more of a spoof. Did they not understand what that show was or what it meant to a generation of school kids who probably shouldn't have been watching it anyway?

First hitting the airways in 1966, it became an after-school obsession of my neighborhood buddies a few years later. I'd come home from school, hurry through homework and snacks and race down the street. We gathered in the Florida room at my neighbor Randy's house (up north, it would be called a "den"). Lounging on pillows on the floor in front of the black-and-white television set with the curtains drawn to make the room as dark as possible, we'd sit riveted as the show was broadcast. The show was in color by the time we were gathering to watch in 1967; however, color television sets were still rare, and I remember the show in black and white.

Dark Shadows was a half-hour show situated in a fictional Northeast town. Collinsport, Maine, was full of vampires, witches, werewolves—you name it. If the character or situation could be considered marginally paranormal, eventually it showed up in the story line. The show was eerie and odd with shadows (natch!) and dramatic music. The characters were always creeping about threatening one another. Barnabas Collins was the big cheese, a two-hundred-year-old vampire who escaped a chained coffin and returned home as a long-lost cousin about six months after the show started airing.

Jacana Way, North Palm Beach, 2014. *Courtesy Berge family collection.*

The plot was as tangled as a European death knot, but once upon a time, I followed it in great detail and could actually explain it. The writers grabbed anything interesting and threw it in the mix. The resulting stew bubbled in our imaginations, causing us all to go to bed on weeknights wide-eyed in the dark.

I couldn't tell you why we gathered at Randy's house to watch it, but I know we never met anywhere else. Every day when the show ended, we emerged into the bright Florida sun, blinking as if we were denizens of the night ourselves. After debating that day's plot corkscrews, we slowly settled into kickball or tag, as if we were normal children, not *Dark Shadows* addicts.

The show ran until 1971. Shot live, microphone booms occasionally appeared at the top of the screen and lines were often flubbed. We absolutely did not care. I didn't get this attached to another show until college, when my sorority sisters and I would almost come to blows as we argued over *General Hospital* versus *One Life to Live*. We scheduled classes around that hour. The wedding of Luke and Laura meant a full house in the TV room that afternoon, but I digress.

If you've never seen the original *Dark Shadows*, I can promise you that it'll appear hokey to you now. Special effects have moved so far beyond what they were in the '60s that what once was terrifying appears laughable. As for the movie, I suppose I will have to see it eventually.

But for now, let me wallow in the remembered terror of the original creepy series watched in a dark room in the middle of the sunny Florida afternoons of my early childhood. Nothing will ever feel quite the same. Perhaps it would make good watching one Halloween season if for nothing else but old time's sake. I wonder if I can round up my old North Palm Beach gang for a *Dark Shadows* reunion.

Randy? Is your Florida room still available?

CHAPTER 25

Sparklers and Moonshine

My family spent most Fourth of July holidays at the North Palm Beach Country Club. Families spread tattered sheets usually used at the beach out along the edges of the fairways as dusk approached. Coolers were frequently raided for cold drinks or youngsters were sent running to the clubhouse for drinks or bags of potato chips. The odor of mosquito repellent hung in the air as we sat patiently waiting, prickly from a day of too much sun at the beach or pool, for the village fireworks to begin. As the sun slowly set, sparklers were lit, and kids carved patterns in the darkening sky. There was always a parent yelling, "Be careful! Those things get hot!" If it wasn't one of my parents, it was one near us.

The moment the sun sank below the horizon, the sky exploded. We leaned back onto the sheets and oohed and ahhed at the elaborate spider webs of light soaring high above us. We could smell the exploded gunpowder as clouds of smoke wafted across the crowd.

In the 1920s, decades before we gathered on the fairways to watch fireworks, the course was used for more than golfing and fireworks. Apparently, when rumrunners weren't smuggling cases of illegal hootch over the nearby waterways, they utilized the clear open areas of the golf course and flew low to deliver contraband. Their cohorts waited in nearby woods to race out and collect the tossed bundles. The area wasn't North Palm Beach then, but the far northern reaches of Kelsey City, now Lake Park. Lawmen were few and far between. It was rumored that some of those sworn to uphold the law were paid to look the other way. In all

Aerial view of North Palm Beach Country Club, 2011. *Courtesy North Palm Beach Country Club.*

Fairway at North Palm Beach Country Club, 2011. *Courtesy North Palm Beach Country Club.*

fairness, times were hard in what was then a primitive tropical paradise, and it wasn't always easy to eke out a living.

In 2012, North Palm Beach again had a "July 4th Red, White and Boom!" celebration at the Country Club at 951 U.S. Highway 1. A free swim in the huge country club pool at noon kicked off the festivities, which were scheduled to continue until 10:00 p.m. with fireworks at 9:00.

If you're lucky enough to live nearby and head over to watch the fireworks, bring your sheet, relax on the lawn and enjoy! As you wave your sparklers waiting for the big show, imagine how it must have looked on a dark, dark night in the 1920s without a house in sight. Hear the uneven drone of the propellers on a smuggler's plane as it exploded out of the darkness and swooped toward the ground so the pilot could toss a package to those waiting below. No need to run for cover, though; this time, the packages are not heading for the ground, but the sky, where they'll explode in celebration of another Fourth of July.

CHAPTER 26

Double Roads

For most children growing up in Palm Beach County, the beach is a constant source of entertainment and enjoyment. During my childhood years in North Palm Beach, we had to travel south to Singer Island or north to Juno Beach and Jupiter to get to the ocean, but the destination was always worth the drive.

In the 1960s and '70s, we had to jump and slide down big sand dunes to reach the surf in Juno Beach. It was an art to avoid the roots of sea grape trees and shrubs and random rocks to keep from falling head over heels. Once on the beach, walking to the surf usually involved a lot of mincing steps in futile attempts to run over the steaming sand, superheated by a glaring sun. My personal favorite involved jumping from towel to towel until I reached cooler, wet sand. I still see people doing the towel-sand hop.

One of our favorite destinations was Double Roads. Literally, a double road for a block or two along A1A just north of Marcinski Road in Juno Beach, Double Roads was a dirt road to the east of two lane A1A. The eastern part of the road was the original U.S. Highway 1. After partially falling into the ocean, U.S. 1 moved west, leaving part of a dirt road behind. I've heard that beach erosion gradually required that bit of dirt road be paved, too. In addition to the paving, sturdy wooden stairways have been installed from the street level to the sand. No more tumbling down dunes.

There was always a bonfire on the beach in the evenings. Then, as now, teenagers liked to socialize without parents, and parties around bonfires were frequent. From the stories friends have shared with me, some were much more exciting than most of the parties I attended. "Submarine races" were as popular then as they are now, and spending the evening cuddled in the dark under blankets beneath the star-speckled sky was pure romance.

Opposite Double Roads, where condominium buildings sit now, boys used to practice their *Dukes of Hazzard* moves in the sand, driving their souped-up cars in wild, wide circles over the sand and scrub. A van even rolled off the road once, toppling over the dune and onto the beach several feet below. No one seems to remember if the van was occupied at the time, but most don't remember anyone being seriously injured.

Crab walks were another evening delight. Seasonally, crabs left the beach in huge numbers and attempted to cross Double Roads and A1A by the light of the moon. Those white bodies scrabbling over the road were enough to give anyone nightmares. Unfortunately, cars kept driving, and the trip became deadly for the crabs. Innocent travelers with their windows down to enjoy the salty sea breeze were treated to the crunch of crabs as pale bodies became easy prey to car tires. The smell of crab parts in undercarriages the following several days were often an unwelcome souvenir of an evening drive by the sea.

When I was camping with the Girl Scouts at Camp Welaka, one of the best field trips for the Scouts was to the beach. The camp would load us into vans and drop us off to walk silently in the dark looking for nesting sea turtles. Once a turtle started laying her eggs, we could turn on flashlights and watch. As the cool, salty breeze blew stiffly off the ocean, we'd stand mute and watch as nature provided the show both on the beach and in the starry sky.

Double Roads is right where it's always been, on A1A just north of Marcinski Road. Still open to the public, it is a great place for a walk on a clear night, but I wouldn't suggest a bonfire. I'm pretty sure you need a permit for that now.

CHAPTER 27

The Intra What?

Have you ever been stuck waiting seemingly endless eons when a drawbridge went up so a tall sailboat could pass by? If you were in eastern Florida at the time, you were likely waiting at a bridge crossing the Intracoastal Waterway.

Running just inside the east coast of Florida from the state line south to Miami is a waterway at various times called "the innercoastal," "the intercoastal" and even the "entercoastal." It's actually the Intracoastal Waterway, and any time someone heads to the beach on the east coast of the entire state of Florida, he or she will pass over it.

When I was a child sailing up and down the Intracoastal in my dad's boat, I thought it was a river. When I spent the summer at Camp Welaka in Tequesta and the Girl Scouts paddled canoes down the north branch of the Loxahatchee River to connect with the Intracoastal, it never occurred to me that in some places the sides were awfully straight. (Frankly, by the time we hit the Intracoastal from North Fork, we were just grateful we had almost reached a landing point. That river is long!) It's kind of close to the ocean, but a river nevertheless. I was right, and I was wrong. The Intracoastal Waterway does have several natural rivers and inlets along it, but they are connected by man-made, dredged thoroughfares of water.

For anyone who takes the time to stop and look at the riverbanks, it becomes obvious that the sides are too straight in some places to be natural. Started in 1883 by the Coast Line Canal & Transportation Company in cahoots with the state of Florida, the waterway was completed from

The Intracoastal from under the Jupiter Bridge facing south, 2013. *Courtesy Berge family collection.*

Jacksonville to Miami in 1912. The man most hold responsible for the development of the east coast of Florida, Henry Flagler, became associated with the company in 1895. He apparently viewed it as a vehicle to help extend his railway down the state.

Before completion of the Intracoastal Waterway, traveling south in Florida wasn't easy. You could sail and hope you didn't get seasick or run into a tropical storm or hurricane. By 1895, you could take one of Henry Flagler's trains. By then, he had managed to extend service all the way to West Palm Beach. A year later, Flagler had extended the railroad to Miami. There were no interstate highways, though, and no turnpike. Military Trail was still more like the military supply trail it started out as rather than the major thoroughfare it is today.

The Atlantic Intracoastal Waterway runs 1,095 miles from Norfolk, Virginia, to Miami, where it meets the Miami River. It may have been completed in the early 1900s, but it wasn't until 1944 that the U.S. Congress agreed to provide the funding to dredge the Jacksonville-to-Miami segment to the same twelve-foot depth as the more northern segment and to deepen the already existing waterway from Miami to Key West.

The Intracoastal facing east, Jupiter, 2013. *Courtesy Berge family collection.*

Why did it become important in 1944? That was when Germans decided to run their Operation Drumbeat along the entire U.S. eastern seaboard, and an alternate route to keep ships moving became urgent. Ships were being hunted and blown up from New York to Key West by German U-boats. With the dredging, smaller boats were able to move to the Intracoastal Waterway, where they were safe despite predators in the ocean.

So the next time you head to one of our wonderful waterfront restaurants and sit under an umbrella gazing out over the very straight Intracoastal Waterway, you now know a few bits of history to astound and amaze your dinner companions.

CHAPTER 28

Where the Pawpaw Grew

When I was a child, Munyon Island was, to me, only one of those interesting bits of land we passed in the Intracoastal on our way to the area around the bigger Peanut Island to the south. The island appeared on the left, a smallish fifteen-acre spit of land covered with Australian pines that swayed in the ocean breeze that crossed the narrow northern end of Singer Island.

In the early 2000s, as an adult with two young children, I took a kayak tour from John D. MacArthur Beach State Park that stopped on Munyon Island. The friend leading the tour walked us all around the island.

A peaceful place, it sits far enough from the population that has encroached on the natural areas of Palm Beach County. As with most places in Palm Beach County, though, there's more to Munyon Island than just an odd name and a quiet place to relax in the middle of a kayak tour.

Munyon Island started out in South Florida history called "Nuctaschoo" Island. The Seminole word referred to the pelicans that claimed the island as home. Palm Beach County History Online says that "a man named Rodgers lived in a tent on the island in 1884," and "the Nathan W. Pitts family purchased the island in 1892, added a two-story house, and developed it into a horticultural paradise."

The fun started in 1901 when a fellow named James Munroe Munyon, nicknamed "Money," purchased the property. Munyon, born in 1847 in Connecticut, was never certified as a physician but peddled "elixirs" that claimed to cure any number of illnesses. He used herbs and roots to create his

Photograph of Dr. James Munyon from front cover of sheet music. *Courtesy Lester R. Levy Sheet Music Collection of the Sheridan Libraries, Johns Hopkins University.*

homeopathic home remedies and spent large amounts of money advertising. His most famous was "Dr. Munyon's Paw-Paw Elixir." It contained fermented pawpaw juice and sulphur water and ended up immortalized in the popular song of the day "Where the Paw Paw Grew." Munyon's pawpaw pills were said to cure biliousness and constipation. In June 1920, chemists from the U.S. government under Pure Food and Drug laws found that Munyon was guilty of having unsubstantiated claims for the wonderful benefits of his products. Two of his magic elixirs were nothing but cane sugar.

But before the trouble in 1903, Munyon built the Hygeia Hotel and added orchards, groves and a seawall. The Hygeia had twenty-one rooms and was five stories tall. Named after the Greek goddess of health, it served as a destination for northerners who came to the island to cure their illnesses. Munyon even had a "Fountain of Youth" on the northern end of the island where a small stone circle sat near the shore. Wealthy visitors to the hotel never knew that Munyon had water piped over from the mainland to bubble up in imitation of a natural spring.

The internationally known Hygeia Hotel burned in 1917, leaving nothing but ruins and the stone Fountain of Youth behind. Two years later, Harry Kelsey, the Boston restaurant entrepreneur who had huge plans for the northern Palm Beach County area, bought around 100,000 acres of prime property. That purchase included Munyon Island. From 1930 to 1950, sand dredged from the Lake Worth Inlet was deposited along the western short of the narrow little island, and gradually, the ruins of the once proud Hygeia Hotel disappeared. The dumping of dredged refuse from the work on the Intracoastal Waterway in the 1930s and '60s had taken its toll, burying the natural wetlands. The island grew to its current forty-five acres.

Ownership of Munyon passed from Harry Kelsey to John D. MacArthur in 1955. MacArthur sold it to the State of Florida in 1981. In 1997, Palm Beach County, along with several state agencies and the West Palm Beach Fishing Club began restoration work that included removal of the Australian pines, which are considered an invasive plant despite the soft, soothing, lovely sound the sea breeze makes when it passes through their branches. When I was there in the early 2000s, the circle of old, weathered stones that had been promoted as Munyon's Fountain of Youth was half buried in the sand on the deserted shoreline, a relic of a con man's dream.

The infamous "Money" Munyon died of apoplexy (called a stroke these days) while dining in Palm Beach at age seventy. Having been divorced from his third wife, Pauline Neff Metzger, an actress he had married in 1908, when he was sixty and she twenty-eight, he left behind only a son and his millions—and of course, his elixirs. His Homeopathic Home Remedy Company continued to operate into the 1940s despite the occasional confiscation of shipments and the imposition of fines by the United States government.

Munyon Island is still an interesting bit of land to pass when boating to points farther south, but these days it also has a boat dock and picnic tables. With the huge attention paid to the replanting of mangroves and other native plants on the island, a trip to Munyon Island is a trip back in time to the Florida that used to exist long before a man named Munyon came around.

CHAPTER 29

Jupiter Lighthouse

From our North Palm Beach home in the 1960s, there wasn't much to see along U.S. 1 beyond an occasional business here or there and acres of vacant land. Through Juno Beach, gently rolling sand dunes covered with native Florida plants appeared on either side of the road, but that was about all there was—until we approached Jupiter. I don't remember that we ever stopped there on our travels. It wasn't far enough away to warrant a restroom or meal break, and Dad just drove through.

At the intersection of U.S. Highway 1 and Indiantown Road, there were a few businesses, but the most exciting site was barely over a mile north. As we approached the bridge that crossed over the Intracoastal by the Jupiter Inlet, we could see the lighthouse rising to our right. Sitting proudly on one of Florida's rare hills, it had started flashing its beacon in 1860 and towered over the surroundings. It still does.

I would have liked to stop and explore the lighthouse back then, but we never did. When I was a teenager, there was always too much going on, and I never took the time. Decades later, my children climbed the stairs of the lighthouse on field trips with their schools, but I was never able to make the climb with their classes.

On a very hot and humid weekend in 2012, I drove over to the lighthouse to do something I'd never done before. I was determined to climb to the top. Luckily for me, the Jupiter Inlet Lighthouse and Museum is operated by the Loxahatchee River Historical Society, whose volunteers and staff members brave the hot weather to lead tours through the grounds and, yes, up to the top of the lighthouse.

Close-up view of Jupiter Inlet Light Station, Palm Beach County, Florida, 1953. *State Archives of Florida, Florida Memory, http://floridamemory.com/items/show/71711.*

I joined a group of adventurers on a Saturday morning tour. Our group was led past the acknowledged oldest home in the area, the Tindall House, which was moved to the grounds from its original location near Center Street. The tour also took us past the Pennock Bell, a relic from Pennock Plantation in old Jupiter. The bell was used in the 1800 and 1900s to communicate with workers in the pineapple fields. To the northeast is an active Coast Guard station because this is still a working lighthouse. Traipsing past native plants and well-tended lawns, our group moved to the star of the show—the Jupiter Lighthouse.

The U.S. government had allocated funds to build a lighthouse on Fort Jupiter Reservation to help the shipping industry after extensive lobbying by the insurance industry. Insurance companies were tired of losses from shipwrecks and had decided that the best way to prevent future wrecks was to build lighthouses along the shoreline of Florida.

This lighthouse was designed by Lieutenant George G. Meade and supplemented by the addition of double walls, porthole windows and extra height courtesy of Lieutenant William Raynolds in 1858. If Meade sounds

View overlooking the marina with Jupiter Inlet lighthouse in the left background, Palm Beach County, Florida. *State Archives of Florida, Florida Memory, http://floridamemory.com/items/show/59227. Photograph by Robert M. Overton.*

familiar to history buffs, that's because Lieutenant Meade later became General Meade, who served in the army of the North in the Civil War. In an odd twist, the Loxahatchee River Historical Society believes a surveyor by the name of Robert E. Lee was one of the team of six surveyors who decided Jupiter Inlet would be a good spot. It's the same Robert E. Lee who later became the general of the Confederate army and for whom Lee County, Florida, is named.

It takes 34 steps to get to the lighthouse base and another 105 to get to the top. Thank heavens there are landings and open windows where sea breezes pour in—that's a rough climb! I can't imagine how the early lighthouse keepers did it several times a day. The view from the top, though, was everything I had imagined. Having pored over history books and pictures of the area, I could imagine how it must have looked when the lighthouse was brand new. It's easy to envision where the inlet was originally located and what the area must have looked like before buildings and paved roads sprouted up like dandelions.

I may not have been successful in talking my dad into stopping by the Jupiter Lighthouse on any of our trips on nearby U.S. Highway 1 in the 1960s, but the delayed climb was worth it and not only because of the catwalk and incredible views. At the top, the original lenses made in France by Fresnel still shine every night as they have almost every night since 1860. A couple of months after the beginning of the Civil War in 1861, enough of the mechanical parts were removed to keep the lighthouse from shining, and it wasn't until June 1866 that the light once again directed sailors safely home.

And that rare hill? Man made. It's actually an Indian midden, or mound. Indians were in and around the inlet area for thousands of years.

CHAPTER 30

Never Found Anywhere Better

The Loggerhead Café is in a two-story building in Carlin Park in Jupiter, Florida. Located just off South SR A1A, it's nothing fancy—an open window in the front so that the bathing-suit crowd can order a sandwich to go, a covered patio in the back for those who want to enjoy the sea air while they dine or have a wet backside from swimming in the nearby ocean and a simple but good menu. That's about it.

The building has been on that spot as long as I can remember. It looks old to the casual observer, although I believe it was built in the 1960s. If there was any doubt that it actually was older than most, the cement bathrooms outside at either end of the building, floors often covered with sand, would be confirmation. The restrooms have been updated, but they're still on the primitive side.

The current building sits on the spot where Captain Charles Carlin ran a lifesaving station from 1885 to 1896 The lifesaving station Carlin built was the first one on the east coast of Florida. Carlin himself passed away in 1912. Carlin had been a British sailor and had served as assistant lighthouse keeper at nearby Jupiter Lighthouse before he moved to the station. At the beginning of World War I, the station merged with the Revenue Cutter Service, and the resulting organization became the U.S. Coast Guard. The original building had to be demolished, but the park still bears his name.

The beach at Carlin Park was one of my family's favorites because of the lifeguards and the handy potties. Somewhere in my box of pictures is one of

Building at Carlin Park, Jupiter, 2013. *Courtesy Berge family collection.*

me at age two in a swimsuit with sunglasses covering blue eyes, posing knee deep in the deep moat around a sand castle.

If one got to the park early enough on a weekend, it was possible to claim possession of one of the pavilions that spread out to the south of the main building like ducks following mama by piling coolers, towels and beach chairs on the cement picnic tables next to the open-air grills. If we weren't grilling lunch ourselves, I'd beg to be allowed to buy a hot dog and a soda at the restaurant window. In 1970, there may have only been 3,136 people in residence in Jupiter, but the population on the beach soared as hundreds more came from inland or north from North Palm Beach and Palm Beach Gardens to enjoy the sun and sand under the watchful eyes of lifeguards. Those pavilions provided a nice bit of shade during breaks from running across the steaming sand hot enough to burn bare feet and swimming in the ice-cold ocean.

After a life of adventure in the navy and around the United States, during which he came home to Jupiter several times, Captain Carlin's grandson, Carlin White, a Jupiter native, returned to serve as mayor and then to retire here. In 2012, I had the pleasure of being included with other Jupiter authors at an event with Mr. White. I didn't want to bother him with all the questions swirling around my brain as it was late in the evening and I was tired by then. I reasoned that since he had recently celebrated his 104th birthday, he might be a little tired, too. I regretted that I had not fought my way through the crowd around him earlier.

After all the authors at the event posed for a group picture, me standing behind Mr. White, I watched as another Jupiter resident grilled him about life in the early years of Jupiter. I don't remember much of the conversation, but I distinctly remember Mr. Carlin's response to the last question. Asked, "Why did you keep coming back to Jupiter?" he answered incredulously, "Why, because I never found anywhere better!"

CHAPTER 31

Who's Toney Penna?

Florida has been a magnet for golfers since the nineteenth century. The mild year-round weather coupled with beautifully designed courses has lured golfers south for decades. The Breakers Hotel built the first eighteen-hole golf course in Florida. According to golf.com, the Breakers links opened in 1896.

Quite a bit north of the Breakers, a little two-lane road in Jupiter named "Toney Penna Drive" runs west from Military Trail (Glynn Mayo Highway, named after Jupiter's first police chief) to Central Boulevard. Not everyone knows who Toney Penna was or how he ended up with a street in Jupiter named after him. I've been told bits and pieces of the Toney Penna story over the years by my dad, but there was more to learn.

Born in Naples, Italy, Anthony Gerald Penna became a well-known golfer beginning with his 1937 win of the Pennsylvania Open Championship. He won no less than four events on the PGA tour, ending with the Atlanta Open in 1947. Toney and his wife, Angela, known affectionately as "Dooks," with their children, daughter Ricky and son Gerry, moved next door to my Aunt Eleanor's house along the Intracoastal Waterway in Delray Beach in 1946. It didn't take my dad and his brother Warren, his main cohort in crime, all of thirteen and fourteen years of age, long to wander the few blocks from their house to check out the new kid, Gerry, and his family. My father's youngest brother, Allen, was too young to be included in these adventures, but from what I've heard, he made up for it in later years. My lips are sealed.

Toney Penna publicity still, 1942. *Wikimedia Commons.*

Penna's son was a year or so younger than my father. I've been told that Gerry, Dad and Warren ended up getting into mischief together more than once. There's a hush-hush tale, long buried in our family lore, about an abandoned building, the three boys, police and bail money. It seems the three boys decided it would be a lot of fun to punch through walls and break some windows in the aforementioned nearby vacant house.

The owner, his name lost to history, discovered the damage, and since Delray Beach was a small town in those days, it didn't take too long before he figured out who was responsible. As a consequence, the three boys were hauled away to the local hoosegow, where they sat miserably waiting for their parents to arrive. My grandparents weren't as well-to-do as the famous golf star, so my grandfather brokered a deal with Penna. Penna would pay the bail money for all three boys, and Dad and Warren would make all of the repairs under their father's supervision. Warren managed to make himself scarce, and my dad and grandfather repaired every bit of the destruction. The boys may have found themselves in more mischief over the next few years, but if they did, those stories must have been buried deeper in the family archives because I've never heard one.

On happier days, Penna carried a small duffel bag filled with golf balls to a local field to practice his drives. After he dumped out the golf balls, Dad and Warren took the empty bag and ran far down the field. Penna swung, and the boys chased all over after balls, gradually filling the bag back up.

As a local celebrity, Penna lived peacefully along the water in Delray, but he had famous friends. He played golf often with singer Perry Como, who first lived in Tequesta Country Club. In later years, Como moved to a house along the Jupiter Inlet in Jupiter Inlet Colony at the northern end of Palm

Front porch of Hartman home, circa 1940s. *Second row, far right*: author's father; *first row, far left*: Gerald Penna; *first row, second from left*: author's uncle Warren Hartman. *Courtesy Hartman family collection.*

Beach County. Penna's golf games with Como had been going on for years before Penna moved to South Florida, partially at Como's suggestion. Back in Delray Beach, it was Penna's visitors who caused quite the sensation. According to Dad, Hollywood luminaries showed up at Penna's house from time to time—Dean Martin and Jerry Lewis among them.

So how did a street in Jupiter, forty-five minutes from Delray, end up being named "Toney Penna Drive?" Penna worked as a representative for MacGregor Golf Company designing clubs until 1967, and in the early 1970s, he went out on his own. He opened a little facility where he manufactured golf clubs he personally designed, eventually holding four patents. Located just east of Military Trail on the south side of what is now known as Toney Penna Drive, the building is still there, but it's been renovated to the point that it's now impossible to tell that, once upon a time, golfing royalty worked there.

Penna died at age eighty-seven in 1995. His son, Gerry, who followed him into the business of golf club design, died in 2006 at age seventy-three. Nathaniel Crosby (yes, Bing's son), who worked for Toney Penna back in the days when Penna himself was still involved, was running Toney Penna Golf in 1992, when Jack Nicklaus decided to enter the business of designing golf clubs. Nathaniel became the president of Nicklaus Golf Equipment, the descendant of the little warehouse Penna built.

If you'd like to get your hands on a Toney Penna club, be prepared to pay. The MacGregor Toney Penna Clubs are extremely rare collectibles. A collector's guide on E-bay says, "An all original, excellent condition set of WWs (white woods) should be worth $1000 or more." The Penna VIP irons (1963–67) are considered so rare it's hard to set a value.

Golf's been a part of the scenery in Florida since the late 1800s. But I'm sure that when Dad and Warren cut through Aunt Eleanor's hedge to get Gerry for yet another adventure, Dad had no idea that Gerry's dad, and later Gerry, would make golf clubs so well designed that devoted golfers still search for and collect them.

CHAPTER 32

Coming Home

It had been a day of Barbie rescuing, running, swimming and hiding and seeking in the large yard full of mango and fruit trees at my grandparents' home in Delray Beach. My cousins and I had run in circles around the huge tree in the middle of the yard until we were dizzy. At least one hundred orchids swayed in the warm summer breeze from the branches overhead.

The men were relaxing by the pool or probably watching a football game on the television console my grandmother had won. My cousin Fred sold her the winning ticket in a sweepstakes, and it was one of the first color televisions in Delray Beach. We were too busy running around outside to watch it most of the time, and this afternoon had been no different. But then, my cousins and I were called in to start helping with Sunday dinner.

"Jack, Freddy, Ruthie, time to come in," Aunt Ann called. We sadly gathered Barbie and her rescuers and trudged to the house. As if marching to our doom, we shuffled our feet and took our time moving through the screen door at the back of the house into the huge farmhouse kitchen.

"Wash your hands and sit over there," Granny said, pointing to one of the two old wooden tables in the kitchen. She placed bowls of freshly washed green beans on the table in front of us. Our job was to snap the ends off what seemed like a never-ending mound of beans.

While we sat and worked on the beans, my cousins and I watched and listened carefully while the women moved in and out of the pantry and around the kitchen. We never heard anything scandalous, but we always paid attention in the hopes that we would.

Touring family on Route A1A, Palm Beach County, Florida, 1960. *State Archives of Florida, Florida Memory, http://floridamemory.com/items/show/78287. Photograph by Charles Barron.*

When the heavy smell of roasting chicken had worked its way into every nook and cranny of the house, Granny called, "Come to dinner, everyone!"

We headed to the big dining room with the sliding glass door that looked over the garden and arranged ourselves around the long table. My grandparents had traveled to Miami to get that table in the 1940s. I was told there were no furniture stores in Palm Beach or Broward counties that carried tables of that size.

Granddad sat at the head of the table. Granny sat next to him so she could get to the kitchen to bring anything else we needed. The platter of roast chicken was placed in front of Granddad. A heaping bowl of mashed potatoes, homemade rolls so delicate they almost floated out of the basket and a huge bowl of the freshly steamed green beans the boys and I just finished snapping were spread out over the length of the table. A pitcher of my grandmother's freshly brewed ice tea sweetened with her just-squeezed lemonade sat sweating on a side table.

A humble prayer followed the arrival of the food, and upon the pronouncement of "Amen!" food and hands flew around the table as the eleven of us reached for the nearest bowl and passed it around.

I was fascinated with the little cut-glass bowls of salt and tiny spoons Granny placed on the table between every other seat. I thought it really grown up to be able to ladle salt over my food, and I tried very hard not to dump any when I delicately filled the little spoon and sprinkled it over my food—bad luck, you know.

My cousins tried to startle me into spilling some occasionally—"BOO!" from Jack and a second later, "HAH!" from Fred. That was about all they could get by with because a stern voice from the head of the table advised them to "stop the nonsense." Both sat straighter and practiced their innocent "who me?" looks.

After everyone had eaten, and we children had cleared the dinner dishes, neatly stacking everything next to the deep kitchen sink, Granddad looked hopefully at Granny.

"What do we have for *gutzel* tonight?" he asked, hands patting his stomach.

We all knew *gutzel* was the word he used for dessert, and our heads turned toward Granny. She smiled, walked into the kitchen and brought a lemon meringue pie, Uncle Allen's favorite, to the table. Everyone smiled. This was good *gutzel.*

Dessert was devoured, the remaining plates cleared and dishes were washed. Dinner over, we slowly took our leave.

With hugs and kisses, more bear hugs from Granddad and punches from the cousins, I climbed into the car with my parents and brother for the long drive home. We never took the western route through the cow pastures as we traveled home. We almost always went straight north on Federal or perhaps Dixie Highway. Often on a clear night, if we were lucky, Dad headed east on Atlantic Avenue until the dead end at A1A with the ocean just beyond. He turned the car north, and I melted into the back seat with the ocean air pouring sweetly through the windows, rolled down to catch whatever breeze the moving car might create. To the east, the moon lit the tops of the gentle swells of the dark waves.

In those days before seat belts, my brother and I lounged on the big back seat with our eyes closed, faces turned to the balmy incoming wind. As we were slowly lulled to sleep, we listened to the click, click, click, clackety-click of the tires on the seamed concrete pavement and the low murmur of our parents' conversation and soft laughter from the front seat as we headed home.

Afterword

Florida is not the same as it was when I was growing up. Part of the difference is that I've grown up, but part of it is that Florida, like everything and everywhere, has changed. Some change has been for the better and some not so much.

The most obvious change is that the population of South Florida has soared. In 1920, when my family had been in Delray about a decade, 18,654 people were estimated to be living in Palm Beach County. In 2010, the U.S. Census estimated that the number of people enjoying the Florida tropics hit a high of 1,320,134. Communities expanded unchecked to the west into the eastern boundaries of the Everglades, the delicate sea of grass that covers most of the southern part of the state. The fragile ecosystem that nurtured the early inhabitants of the state has been altered irrevocably. Areas that should have remained a natural wilderness have been paved to accommodate the burgeoning development.

As I head north on A1A today, and look west, I can see buildings that have changed the skyline. But if I look to the east, the ocean is unchanged.

It's the same as when Indians braved the surf to fish or pulled tarpon from the Loxahatchee River in Jupiter. It's the same as when storms wrecked Jonathan Dickinson's ship in 1696, and pirate ships and Spanish galleons met their dooms just offshore. It's the same as when my father was a lifeguard on the ocean in Delray Beach in the 1950s. It's the same as when I swam a quarter mile out to sea with the theme song to the movie *Jaws* running through my head to earn my senior lifesaving certificate in the 1970s. It's the same as when my children built their first sandcastle on the beach in Jupiter in the 1990s. And it's the same today.

Thank you for joining me on this trip home. I hope my memories helped spark some of yours and brought a smile to your face.

Let me fold the blanket, and we'll leave the sound of the surf behind us as we walk back up the wooden stairs from the beach to A1A. We'll brush the sand off our feet and climb back into today.

Bibliography

American Business Leaders of the Twentieth Century. http://www.hbs.edu/leadership/database/leaders/jules_s_bache.html (accessed July 4, 2013).

Benton, Claudet. *Footprints in Time*. N.p.: self-published, 1989.

———. *The Outdoor Experience: Wildflowers of Welaka*. 100th anniversary edition. N.p.: self-published, 2012.

Branch, Chas. A. Undated manuscript. North Palm Beach Public Library and the Historical Society of Palm Beach County.

A Brief History of Air Conditioning. www.popularmechanics.com (accessed September 29, 2013).

Britt, Ryan. "A *Dark Shadows* Crash Course." Science Fiction, Fantasy, The Universe. May 2012. www.tor.com/blogs (accessed August 29, 2013).

CD of the script presented to the Palm Beach Gardens Historical Society at program on December 9, 2009. Read by Kelly Chase. Produced by Don Kiselewski.

Clint Walker: The Big Guy Himself. www.clintwalker.com (accessed April 24, 2012).

Clough, Bryan. "Dr. Crippen: The Most Infamous Murderer in Anglo-American Relations." www.drcrippen.co.uk (accessed August 10, 2013).

Coast Guard Station Lake Worth Inlet, Peanut Island, Palm Beach and Riviera Beach. Florida aerial and regular photos gallery. www.pbase.com/airlinerphotos (accessed October 10, 2011).

Community: About Us. www.palmbeachschools.org (accessed May 21, 2012).

Courier Highlights. "Jupiter Inlet." May 23, 1974, 137. Courtesy of Historical Society of Palm Beach County.

Dark Shadows. TV series 1966–1971. IMDb. www.imdb.com (accessed October 3, 2012).

Dark Shadows. www.vmomovies.weebly.com (accessed August 29, 2013).

Detwiller, Paula. "Lake Ida: From Swampland to Settled Neighborhood." *Lake Ida Current* (Spring 2011). www.lakeidadelray.com (accessed June 10, 2012).

DiPaolo, Bill. "North Palm Beach Elementary Students Displaced for Two Years While School Is Built." *Palm Beach Post*. June 22, 2012. http://www.palmbeachpost.com/news/news/ (accessed September 5, 2012).

DuBois, Bessie Wilson. "Jupiter Inlet." Reprinted from *Tequesta* in *Journal of the Historical Association of Southern Florida* 28 (1968): 19–35.

"Fish! South Florida Canals: Angler's Guide to Earman River Canal (C-17) Palm Beach County." http://myfwc.com/media (accessed June 15, 2011).

"Florida State Parks 75th Anniversary 1935–2010. John D. MacArthur Beach State Park." www.floridastateparks.org (accessed June 4, 2012).

"Florida Surfing.com Regions." http://floridasurfing.com (accessed February 6, 2012).

Forstall, Richard L. Population Division, U.S. Bureau of the Census. *Population of Counties by Decennial Census: 1900 to 1990*. Washington, D.C., 1995.

Fuchs, Dale. "Lake Park Cuts Parade from Budget." *Palm Beach Post*, September 8, 1993.

———. "Parade Approval Comes Too Late for Lake Park." *Palm Beach Post*, October 28, 1993.

Geinger, Viola. "Bottle Thrown at Children's Dance Group." *Palm Beach Post*, December 14, 1992.

Hartman, Norman G., retired. Interview with the author. Several dates throughout 2012.

Hebert, Paul J. "Atlantic Hurricane Season of 1979." *Monthly Weather Review* 108, no. 7 (July 1, 1980): 973–90. Accessed December 1, 2012.

"Hetzel Brothers Christmas." Palm Beach County Archives. http://pbgarchives.org/items/show/108 (accessed January 11, 2002).

Historic Palm Beach by the *Palm Beach Post*. "This Week in History: Good Samaritan Hospital Opens in West Palm Beach." www.historicpalmbeach.com (accessed April 24, 2012).

"The History of Singer Island." www.singerisland.com (accessed August 29, 2013).

The History of Terrazzo. www.arcadianflooring.com (accessed March 1, 2012).

History: Palm Beach Medical Society. www.pbcms.org (accessed April 24, 2012).

Howard, William. "Lake Park Christmas Parade in Doubt Again After '92 Brawl." *Palm Beach Post*, April 6, 1993.

———. "Lake Park Keeps Christmas in Dixie Parade." *Palm Beach Post*, April 8, 1993.

Hughes, John. "Jingle Bells Ring in the Fights, Thieves, Drugs." *Sun Sentinel*, December 24, 1992. sunsentinel.com (accessed December 30, 2013).

I Love Lake Park, Florida page. www.facebook.com (accessed August 25, 2011).

"Juno Dunes History." www.pbcgov.com (accessed January 9, 2012).

Kleinberg, Eliot. "Historic Palm Beach. Singer Island Once Home to Popular Nude Beach." Posted August 7, 2002. www.historicpalmbeach.com (accessed June 4, 2012).

———. "Kelsey City Arch Ruined in 1928 Hurricane." August 2004. http://www.historicpalmbeach.com (accessed September 20, 2011).

Kriplen, Nancy. *The Eccentric Billionaire*. New York: Amacom, American Management Association, 2008.

"Lake Worth Lagoon." Undated brochure. Peanut Island Environmental Enhancement. www.lwli.org. Palm Beach County Board of Commissioners, Palm Beach County Department of Environmental Resources Management and Department of Parks and Recreation, Peanut Island Park & Campground, Palm Beach Maritime Museum.

"Lighthouse Drive over North Palm Beach Waterway." http://uglybridges.com (accessed January 13, 2012).

Loxahatchee River Historical Society. Tour of lighthouse grounds and lighthouse. September 2012.

"MacArthur Beach State Park Dune News." Newsletter Fall/Winter 2009. www.macarthurbeach.org (accessed May 13, 2012).

McEvoy, George. "Go Hide, You Moral Busybodies." *Palm Beach Post*, June 18, 1990.

McGoun, William E. *Southeast Florida Pioneers: The Palm and Treasure Coasts*. Sarasota, FL. Pineapple Press, Inc., 1998.

Mosquito Information Site. http://mosquito.ifas.ufl.edu (accessed June 9, 2012).

"Munyon Island." www.pbcgov.com (accessed August 10, 2013).

Norris, Tim. "Our Canals." *Palm Beach Gardens and Jupiter Florida Weekly*. Posted September 13, 2012. http://palmbeachgardens.floridaweekly.com/news/2012-09-13/Top_News/Our_Canals.html (accessed December 5, 2012).

"Nude Beaches, Resorts, Associations & News from Florida and around the World." www.thepalmbeachtimes (accessed June 4, 2012).

"Obituary. Jerome V. Kelly." www.kellyfamilynetwork.com (accessed November 1, 2011).

Ostrowski. Jeff. "What Economic Slide? Water Park Buys Site." *Palm Beach Post*, July 30, 2010.

Palm Beach County History Online. "Earman, Florida." www.pbchistoryonline.org/page/earman (accessed June 15, 2011).

———. "Jupiter Inlet Lifesaving Station." www.pbchistoryonline.org (accessed January 17, 2012).

———. "Jupiter." www.pbchistoryonline.org (accessed August 29, 2013).

Palm Beach County School Construction History. http://www.palmbeachschools.org/planning/FYP2012/documents/FY2011-FY2015Five-YearPlanandCapitalBudget.PDF.

Palm Beach Gardens Historical Society. www.pbghistoricalsociety.org (accessed January 11, 2012).

Palm Beach Post. "Christmas Parade Head Quietly Quits in Lake Park." September 3, 1990.

———. December 15, 1986.

———. "Don't Do an About-Face." January 19, 1993.

———. "Fine Ocean Property Sold to Paris Singer." June 19, 1918. Archives of the Historical Society of Palm Beach County.

———. March 6, 1926.

———. "Paris Singer Purchases Still Another Valuable Water Front." April 4, 1918. Archives of the Historical Society of Palm Beach County.

———. "Singer Obtains $1,500,000 More Beach to North." June 4, 1925. Archives of the Historical Society of Palm Beach County.

———. "$6,000 Gift May Save Holiday Parade." October 23, 1993.

Palm Beach Times. "Arnold Given Seminole Job." May 25, 1929. Archives of the Historical Society of Palm Beach County.

———. "Seminole Club Bids Received." May 23, 1929. Archives of the Historical Society of Palm Beach County.

———. "Seminole Club Will Open on Dec. 24th." November 24, 1932. Archives of the Historical Society of Palm Beach County.

———. "Seminole Golf Club Added to Attractions at Resort." March 30, 1929. Archives of the Historical Society of Palm Beach County.

———. "Singer Plans Big Developments on New Inlet Holdings." August 21, 1925. Archives of the Historical Society of Palm Beach County.

Parkman, Aubrey. "The Intracoastal Waterway from Beaufort, North Carolina, to Key West, Florida." *History of the Waterways of the Atlantic Coast of the United States*. National Waterways Study, January 1983. U.S. Army Engineer Water Resources Support Center, Institute for Water Resources, 74–75.

———. "The Intracoastal Waterway, Jacksonville to Miami, Florida." *History of the Waterways of the Atlantic Coast of the United States*. National Waterways Study, January 1983. U.S. Army Engineer Water Resources Support Center, Institute for Water Resources, 83–87.

Pickel, Brad. AIWA: The Voice of the Waterway. "About Us." Updated Wednesday, March 23, 2011. www.atlanticintracoastal.org (accessed August 30, 2013).

Pounds, Stephen. "Spurned Love Sets Off Melee." *Palm Beach Post*, December 15, 1992.

Procyk, Richard. *The Loxahatchee Lament*. Vol. 1. Jupiter, FL: Cary Publishing, Inc., 1978.

Rance, Caroline. "Munyon Is Ready…Would You Buy a Homeopathic Remedy from This Man?" http://thequackdoctor.com/index.php/munyon-is-ready (accessed December 30, 2013).

Reis, John R. "The Life & Times of Jonathan R. Dickinson." Text of a speech given September 21, 1996. www.apex-ephemera.com (accessed February 16, 2012).

Schwem, Greg. "Spectators Enjoy 'Christmas in Dixie.'" *Palm Beach Post*. September 9, 1982.

Snyder, James D. *Five Thousand Years on the Loxahatchee*. Jupiter, FL: Pharos Books, 2003.

"The Story of Jonathan Dickinson." University of Florida George A. Smathers Libraries. http://ufdc.ufl.edu (accessed February 16, 2012).

SunSentinel.com. "Biggest Palm Myths Debunked." Fairchild's Tropical Garden Column. August 26, 2012, 5G.

———. "100 Years of Girl Scouts." March 11, 2012, 16A.

Taylor, Dick. "Eggs A-la Como for Toney's Gal." *Palm Beach Post*, January 29, 1956.

"Town History Past and Present." www.palmbeachshores.fl.us (accessed August 29, 2013).

"Town of Jupiter History Guest Book." www.jupiter.fl.us/programs (accessed January 17, 2012).

"Town of Jupiter." www.jupiter.fl.us (accessed January 17, 2012).

Tropical Sun. "Ocean Front Tract Is Sold." February 20, 1925. Archives Historical Society of Palm Beach County.

"2003 Palm Beach County, A History of Palm Beach County Inlets." http://www.palmbeachshoresfl.us (accessed August 10, 2013).

U.S. Army Corps of Engineers. "Atlantic Intracoastal Waterway." www.nao.usace.army.mil (accessed August 29, 2013).

Van Gieson, John. "Poor Amaryllis is stuck on Florida." *St. Petersburg Times*, July 31, 1966. Online archives accessed August 1, 2012.

"Walk Softly on Our World." Book published by the Girl Scout Council of Southeast Florida. Undated.

We Grew Up in North Palm Beach! page. www.facebook.com (accessed November 8, 2011).

Wheeler, Ryan J., Wm. Jerald Kennedy and James P. Pepe. http://ufdc.ufl.edu/UF00027829/00090/2j "Special Issue: The Archaeology of Jupiter Inlet and Coastal Palm Beach County." *Florida Anthropologist* 55, no. 3–4 (September–December 2002). Accessed July 4, 2013.

World Golf Hall of Fame. http://www.worldgolfhalloffame.org/hof/member.php?member=110 (accessed July 4, 2013).

www.rapidswaterpark.com (accessed June 8, 2012).

You Know You're From Palm Beach County If… page. www.facebook.com (accessed June 4, 5 and 7, 2012).

Index

M

N

O

P

W

Z

About the Author

A history geek since childhood, Ruth Hartman Berge enjoyed listening to her parents, grandparents and aunts and uncles talk about the "good ol' days" when Palm Beach County was mostly cow pastures, farm lands and pineapple fields. A member of Mensa, she is a former member of the board of directors of the Writers' Network of South Florida and also was a columnist for Seabreeze Publications, Inc., where her column, The Florida You Don't Know, enjoyed a wide and loyal readership. Currently, in addition to working on her first mystery novel, she writes a blog at ruththewriter.blogspot.com about whatever grabs her attention. Oftentimes, the topic is some little-known fact about her Palm Beach County surroundings.

Ruth was born in West Palm Beach and spent most of her life in Palm Beach County. Aside from forays to Tallahassee, where she graduated from Florida State University, Ruth's home base has remained in the county she finds so fascinating. She has two wonderful children and is currently owned by three cats, one of whom is disabled and was the inspiration for her children's book, *Betty Tales: The True Story of a Brave Bobblehead Cat*. A voracious reader, she enjoys writing in several different genres but finds herself drawn time and time again to stories that evoke the forgotten paradise of the Florida that existed in the past.